The
Winning
Edge

The author and a friend enjoying each other's company.   *Sharon Wohlmuth*

The Winning Edge

Show Ring Secrets

GEORGE G. ALSTON
with
CONNIE VANACORE

HOWELL BOOK HOUSE

New York

Maxwell Macmillan Canada
Toronto

Maxwell Macmillan International
New York   Oxford   Singapore   Sydney

Howell Book House
Macmillan Publishing Company
866 Third Avenue
New York, NY 10022

Maxwell Macmillan Canada, Inc.
1200 Eglinton Avenue East
Suite 200
Don Mills, Ontario M3C 3N1

Macmillan Publishing Company is part of the Maxwell Communication Group of Companies.

Library of Congress Cataloging-in-Publication Data

Alston, George G.
    The winning edge: show ring secrets/George G. Alston with Connie Vanacore.
        p.   cm.
    ISBN 0-87605-834-9
    1. Dogs—Showing.   2. Dog shows.   I. Vanacore, Connie.
II. Title.
SF425.A47   1992
636.7'088'8—dc20   91–31433
                                                           CIP

Macmillan books are available at special discounts for bulk purchases for sales promotions, premiums, fund-raising, or educational use. For details, contact:

Special Sales Director
Macmillan Publishing Company
866 Third Avenue
New York, NY 10022

10 9 8 7 6 5 4 3 2

Printed in the United States of America

To my teachers, those who knowingly taught me and those who unknowingly taught me.

Thank you.

Contents

Foreword

IN LOOKING BACK over more than half a century in dogs, a lot of names are part of the past. Some flash back because of something said or done to remind you. A few always remain because of indelible memories, but these are very few in the legions that have marched across the dog show stage. And those few have had some quality, some unique essence, that lifted them above the rest.

George Alston is one of these. He has been a great handler. Greatness in the handling profession means that you have a fine kennel, know how to select top dogs for the ring, know how to present them and know how to win or lose gracefully.

But for me, those of indelible memory have had something more. I think of Percy Roberts, the boy who came to America and whose phenomenal memory made him one of the most successful dog importers of all time. I think of Harry Sangster, whose life was cut short just before he could start his judging career.

George Alston belongs with these because of his own special qualities. He had the courage to "bench" himself when he realized he needed a rest. Now he has the courage to start a new life as a writer, teacher and lecturer. Very few would dare to change their lives so radically at any age. But George has these other special qualities. He is a brilliant speaker, one who adds humor to great knowledge. He is a teacher who can call upon his vast knowledge to be effective.

Maxwell Riddle

Introduction

THIS BOOK is written for the amateur exhibitor who already knows the basics of showing a dog. It is directed toward those amateurs who are truly interested in the sport of dogs, and who plan to hone their skills to win more consistently in the show ring.

The information given in this book is the result of my experience as a professional handler, spanning a career of forty years. It is an outgrowth of lectures that I have given to thousands of amateurs who wish to learn the finer points of showing a dog.

Showing dogs is the only sport that, by the payment of an entry fee and with no training whatsoever, you can compete directly with a professional. There is no other organized sport in which you can do that.

You, as an amateur, are competing against someone who makes a livelihood from showing dogs. You are competing with a professional who has dedicated his or her life to this sport, who has spent many years in apprenticeship learning the trade. Yet, you, as an amateur, will compete in the same arena for the same awards.

In order to do this successfully, you have to have the same enthusiasm for it. You have to have the same dedication. How many people during the last year, seven days a week, 365 days a year, did something to improve their abilities showing dogs? The professionals do this for a living. How are you going to beat them? Or even catch up, if they keep working to improve their skills and you don't? These are the cold, hard facts.

WHAT THE JUDGE SEES IS WHAT YOU GET

A judge can only judge what is presented in the ring. The American Kennel Club allows a judge approximately a minute and a half per dog. The judge cannot wait to assume. He or she must judge what is seen. If you do not present what the judge wants to see, you are going to lose. So you must learn to present your dog as efficiently as possible in the least amount of time. It takes work, practice and dedication.

Professionals weren't born with a lead in their hands. It is an unnatural thing to run around in a circle inside of baby gates in the rain and the snow and the mud while dressed in a jacket and tie. You drive all night and you sleep in the car and you eat fast food for the pleasure of showing a dog, so you might as well give yourself an advantage and do it right.

When the judge comes to the end of the class and tries to make a decision, if the professional handler has the dog set up right and the owner handler the dog set up wrong, who wins? The professional will, nine times out of ten. Yet the owner will stand there and complain that the professional always wins.

Amateurs have a great advantage, if they will use it to their own benefit. They usually have only one dog to show, so they have the time to train that dog, condition it, learn about its strong and weak points and practice showing under all kinds of circumstances. Therefore, when they go into the ring, there should be no surprises.

The professional must handle a great many dogs in the course of the day, some of whom the handler may not know very well, yet that handler is expected to make each one look like a million dollars.

Who has the advantage under those conditions?

The purpose of this book is to help the amateur with one show dog to gain the winning edge in the show ring.

1

The Perfect Handler

THERE ARE all kinds of handlers in this world. There are good ones, bad ones, responsible ones and ring jockeys, who don't care a damn about the dogs they handle. Then there is the perfect handler.

INVISIBILITY

The perfect handler is invisible. But how can that be? Well, you should be able to watch a Best in Show lineup, walk away from the ring and say to your friends, "That was an absolutely gorgeous dog that went Best in Show. Who handled it?"

Sometimes you will overhear the ringside talk and catch someone saying, "Boy, that's a good handler. Look at him work!" If you are aware that a handler is working, that person is not doing his or her best, or to put it a little more kindly, those handlers are not as good as they could be.

The handler should fade into the background, putting the dog forward with a minimum of hand motions. The judge should think that this dog is doing it all alone, and if you have worked with your

This young man is dressed in jacket and tie despite the heat.

Exhibitors' clothing should contrast with their dogs, but in a subtle manner.

dog, and know the right moves to make to enable the dog to show off, you will be invisible.

A good handler does not continually fuss with the dog, move around the dog, adjust its position, stroke, push, pull or poke at it or draw the judge's eye away from the dog itself at any time.

A good handler does not constantly smile, grin or talk to the judge to get attention. Judges hate exhibitors who fawn over them in the ring, pleading and begging with their eyes for the win. Pay attention to your dog and allow the judge to demonstrate being capable of finding the best one in the ring without your prodding.

Being invisible involves dressing for the occasion, too. Ladies should not try to attract the judge in the ring by wearing low-cut blouses with nothing underneath. It may make for good ringside gossip, but it detracts from the dog. Do not wear colors that constantly draw the judge's eye away from the dog. Most judges prefer to concentrate on the job at hand, and distractions cut into the two minutes or less that they have to examine your dog.

Men should wear conservative clothes, too. Loud jackets and plaid pants may make a fashion statement, but not to a judge who is interested in seeing your dog.

At the other extreme, do not wear clothes that allow the dog to blend into the background. If you have a black dog, do not wear a black top or a black skirt, unless you really wish to hide the dog completely from the judge's view. Wear colors that contrast subtly with your dog, without calling attention to you.

Another faux pas of dressing involves ladies who wear bangle bracelets that clang as they move. They distract or even spook other dogs in the ring. This is inconsiderate and impolite. Along the same lines are men who carry pockets full of change that jingle as they run. One handler's children always seemed to be conveniently around just before the first class of the day when dad emptied his pockets, providing them with money for the concession stands.

ADAPTABILITY

If the definition of the perfect handler is invisibility, the greatest attribute that a handler can have is the ability to adapt.

The reason that adaptability is so important is that at no time will you ever show the same dog exactly the same way twice, even

The handler must create the perfect picture each and every time the dog is shown.

on the same day. During judging of the breed, the Group and Best in Show, the dog is going to react to its environment differently. At every level there will be different competition, different judges, different ring conditions. You must be able to adapt to those changes so that it looks to everybody else like the dog is doing exactly the same thing every single time. You will handle your dog in a small ring differently than in a big one during Group competition, for instance. The ground conditions may be different in the morning, when there is dew on the grass, than in the afternoon, when the sun has baked the grass into a slick dust patch. You must know how to adapt to those changing conditions at the same time that you must be able to read the dog's mood. Is your dog happier in the morning than in the afternoon? Does the dog do better in the cold or the heat? Some dogs love the rain. Others act as though they would melt away if a drop fell on them. You must prepare yourself to adapt to all those variables.

Part of being adaptable is to have your dog trained to respond in different ways to different conditions. Later in this book we will talk about training your dog to respond to every aspect of the show ring.

CONSISTENCY

At the same time that you and your dog are adapting to changing conditions, you must show so that your dog consistently appears in the same way, so that the dog's performance looks the same to the judge, even though you know that you are handling differently. Your dog must look the same in the Group and Best in Show ring as it did in the breed ring, and it must handle in the same top form.

Remember that you may possibly be gaited once, twice, three times in the Group ring. When you are in that competition, the judge is looking for one goof. In my classes we play a game: one goof and you're out. That's about the way it is when you're playing with the big kids in the ring.

The most *difficult* thing in showing a dog is to be consistent in the way you show it. Once you have learned to do any one thing correctly, you must do it correctly every single time thereafter. That takes practice, practice and more practice, until the moves become second nature. In my beginner classes I make my students set up their dogs in ten seconds, and they must practice until they can do it perfectly every time. If you have to fuss with your dog every time you set it up, you are wasting valuable seconds in which your dog should be showing off, looking its best.

THE HANDLER AS ARTIST

When you are in the ring showing a dog, you are an artist. You are creating a picture, usually an unnatural picture, because you will be emphasizing the dog's assets and attempting to hide its faults. You are trying to sell something to the judge. When you take the legs and place them a certain way, yank up the head and pull the tail in the air, you are molding that dog into a position that you consider looks good to the judge.

In order to create the picture that you want with that dog, you must know its good points and its faults. You must have studied your dog standing and gaiting so that you are familiar with all its parts. You must practice showing off the dog's good points so that the judge sees what *you* want to be seen.

Just as an artist creates an illusion on canvas or paper, the handler creates an illusion for the judge. Professional handlers know how to show to the judge those qualities that they wish the judge to see. Owner-handlers must practice in order to create the picture that they wish to present to the judge.

The difference between artists and dog show exhibitors is that when artists create a work, such as a sculpture, they do it once and it is done for all time. They never have to do that piece again. If they want a copy of it, they make a mold, cast it in bronze, plastic, brass or whatever material they choose. If artists make a painting or an engraving, they can make prints of that, but they never have to go back and create the original work of art again.

When you show a dog, you must create the same picture of that dog every time it is shown. Every time you stack a dog, it must look the same. Every time you gait a dog, it must look the same, and it must be as perfect a picture as you can make it.

Remember consistency. Owner-handlers often walk into the ring and stack their dog, and it is perfect. But the next time, maybe three minutes later, its feet are going in four different directions. One goof and the professional wins! It does not take magic to stack

This handler is presenting the head as if it was a work of art.

In many parts of the country, shows are held outdoors on grass all year 'round, which makes creating a consistent picture somewhat easier.

and gait perfectly and consistently every time. It does take work, effort and patience to do the job right.

Patience is a commodity that many owner-handlers seem to lack. They want to win immediately, without having to learn the sport, study their breeds or put in the time needed to properly train and condition their dogs. In order to win regularly, you cannot be one of those.

PRIDE

In order for someone to be able to put enough heart and soul into showing a dog perfectly every weekend (or whenever they take it into the ring), that person must believe in the dog. A handler, whether amateur or professional, must have faith that this is a good dog, worthy of being shown, worthy of winning. You must have pride in your animal, and you must treat it with respect and make that pride evident to the judge.

Just as artists take pride in their work, you must take pride in presenting your dog as if it were the best animal you have ever seen and that you are doing the judge a favor to allow her to put her hands on this valuable animal.

Exhibitors who manhandle their dogs, pulling them around, grabbing them by the muzzle or yanking them here and there, are saying that this is just a piece of meat. If they have no pride in their dog, why should the judge?

Consider a collector of china and porcelain. When you go to visit the collection, the owner grabs a beer mug from the shelf and says, "I got this at the local saloon." You will notice that there is no particular care taken in handling this piece of china. "But this one," the collector says, "is very rare and beautiful. See the lines and the translucent quality." This porcelain is held gently with the fingertips. It is presented to you with the greatest care so that you can admire its value.

When you present your dog to the judge, you must take as much care as that collector did with the china. If you do not believe that your dog is a precious commodity, get a different attitude, or a different dog.

You will often hear professional handlers talk about their top dogs as being animals that are important to their breeds, or that they are worthy of being shown because of their quality. Most good professional handlers who campaign a dog for two or three years genuinely believe in that dog. They are not going to invest the time and energy, or their clients' money, in a dog in which they do not have pride.

Owner-handlers must have faith in their animals, also, in order to do them justice in the ring. In fact, because they usually have a small number of dogs to show, they should possess and demonstrate even greater respect than the professional.

This concept of the handler as artist, collector and caretaker of the dog will often make the difference between being able to present a dog consistently at its best and consistently winning, or losing to the competition who may be showing a dog not as good as yours.

Anyone can handle a dog. But it takes skill to present one so that judges think this is the greatest specimen of the breed that they have ever seen and they are honored to have it in their ring.

Ch. McCamon Marquis in top condition and showing the genetic heritage and good care necessary to become a winner in the show ring.

2

The Right Stuff—
The Making of a
Show Dog

SHOW DOGS are made, not born. It is not natural for dogs to love to run around in a circle, stand without moving, have strange people put their hands all over them, ride for days in crates and exercise in tiny pens. They have to be taught to love it, to be happy to be in the show ring, to live for the moment that the show lead comes out and it is time to play show dog.

Dogs are just like people. If they enjoy doing something, they will do it with enthusiasm. If they don't enjoy something, they won't do it willingly. They will try to get out of it, just like kids at school. Some kids are lucky enough to have good teachers. A good teacher brings out the best in a student, and the student will try to do anything to please that teacher. In the process the student will learn to enjoy school. It's the same thing showing dogs. You teach them to enjoy it. And if you do not, the most magnificent dog in the world will not make a good show dog.

GENETICS

It is almost too basic to say, but you'd be surprised at how many people come into the show ring with a really mediocre dog. In order to win, you have to have a decent dog. Unless the basic structure is there, you are wasting your money and your time in trying to campaign that dog. Take it home and love it, and if you are truly interested in showing dogs, go buy yourself a good dog. Know your breed. Get the best dog that you can afford, but especially one that has no major faults. Judges may not know the finer points of every breed, but even the worst of them can spot cow hocks, missing teeth or yellow eyes on a breed where the standard calls for dark ones, and so forth.

Dog shows were developed to be a showcase for breeding stock. Although that idea may take a backseat to the more obvious search for wins, owner-handlers particularly should pay attention to genetic faults. Don't waste your money trying to campaign a dog with serious genetic problems, even though they may be hidden from view. When that dog or bitch is bred, those faults will appear, and your reputation will take a nose dive. Owner-handlers, who generally are also breeders, do control the fate and the direction a breed takes over the years. It is fine to hone your skills as a handler, but do it with a dog that is good for the breed. The whole idea is to improve the breeds, is it not?

Be truthful to yourself when evaluating your dog for the show ring. This is where the professional has an advantage, because he or she is not wrapped up in the personality of the dog. You have to be coldhearted when looking at your dog as a prospective Group or Best in Show winner.

You also have to keep looking at your dog as it grows older. The animal that looks good at one year may be excellent at eighteen months and over the hill at three. On the other hand, some breeds do not mature until they are two or three years old, and it is helpful to the owner-handler to know the lines that the dog comes from in order to know what to anticipate as far as a show career is concerned.

The other necessity for a show dog, besides good conformation, is good temperament. The life of a show dog is rigorous. A dog that is flaky, shy, aggressive or unstable will not make a good Specials dog over the long haul. Sure, there are things that can be done to compensate for undesirable traits, but many are ethically

14

wrong or not good for the dog. It is up to the breeders and owner-handlers to produce animals that are sound in mind and body, and then to take those dogs and make them into winners. If people are not honest, the sport of dogs won't be around very long.

GOOD HEALTH—A MUST

A show dog must be a healthy dog. That begins from the time it comes into your home.

Number one, get yourself a good veterinarian, one that will listen to the lay person. One that is not in love with the degree. That may be a tall order, but you have to get one who will listen to you as a dog person, because you are relating symptoms. If you are working with your dog every day, as you should be if you want to beat the professional handlers, you should know immediately if your dog is not right. You must be able to communicate with your veterinarian, and your vet should be willing to listen to you.

Internal Parasites

Dogs must be worm free, and all puppies should be checked regularly. Once they are pronounced free of parasites and the dog is being shown, stools should be analyzed once a month. If you suspect that your dog has parasites, but nothing shows in a single stool sample, take readings on three consecutive days at different times of the day.

If your dog has been treated for worms, your veterinarian may recommend that you repeat the treatment two or three weeks later, depending upon the life cycle of the particular parasite. This is to eliminate additional worms that may hatch from larvae untouched by the parasiticide.

Intestinal parasites have a devastating effect on the dog's general health and well-being, so it is extremely important that they be taken care of on a regular basis.

External Parasites

Fleas are probably the cause of most coat and skin problems. Some dogs may be flea-allergic, where one bite from a flea can send the dog into a frenzy of biting, scratching and chewing. All dogs can suffer from fleas. Depending on the climate, fleas can be either a minor inconvenience or a major headache. In the southeast, flea control is a vitally important part of keeping show dogs in condition. It requires constant attention—dipping, spraying and bombing the house, the kennel and the yard in order to keep ahead of the problem. This must be done if you ever intend to have a dog in good show coat.

There are other parasites that can ruin your dog's coat and general health. In some parts of the country, *chiggers, lice* and *mites* get into the coat and skin. In almost all parts of the country ticks have taken control. *Lyme disease* is the cause of serious illness in both dogs and human beings. In dogs, lameness, fever, lack of energy and anorexia may all be symptoms of Lyme disease carried by deer ticks. If left untreated, the parasite may migrate into the joints, causing permanent arthritic damage. The nervous system, heart, lungs and brain may all be affected by an infestation of the parasite that causes Lyme disease.

There are other tick-borne diseases, such as *Rocky Mountain spotted fever* and *babesia*. These are carried by the brown dog tick or the wood tick. Their prevalence depends upon where you live.

Skin Conditions

One of the most devastating skin diseases is *demodectic mange*. It can infect any dog, but there is a genetic component that makes some breeds more susceptible to it than others. Doberman Pinschers have a high incidence of demodectic mange. It causes severe itching, crusting of the skin and hair loss. It is a treatable disease, but veterinarians recommend to their clients that those dogs affected not be bred.

Many skin diseases are thought to have a genetic component. As breeders you should be aware that many breeds are affected with different skin problems. Besides keeping veterinarians in business, there is no good reason for perpetuating a line of dogs that produces more dogs with skin problems. These dogs are practically impossible to keep in show condition, and you as owner-handler are wasting your money and your energy trying to maintain a dog with an inherent skin condition as a top show contender. Why would you want to anyway?

DIET

Diet is the next most important element in your dog's health.

As a general rule you want a good commercial dog food without a lot of extras in it. There are dog foods designed for every stage of life and every type of activity a dog can find itself in. Show dogs are not out working in the field every day, nor are they mushing on the Iditarod. You do not want a food with a lot of additives, nor do you want to supplement the food with a lot of stuff the dog doesn't need. The reputation of a professional handler depends on the condition a dog is in whenever it goes into the ring. If the dogs are in poor condition, they and the handlers lose. And if handlers lose often enough, they are out of business. Ask professionals whom you trust what they feed their dogs, and follow their suggestions. See if they work for you. You have to know your dog and maintain it on the best diet for that individual. If you find one that works well, don't keep changing around, trying this and that. You'll never know what is successful unless you keep on it for a period of time.

There are some dogs that because of specific problems have to be on specialized diets. Food allergies are not uncommon, and can be devastating to a dog's coat and general health. Consult with your veterinarian about allergy testing before changing from one diet to another.

HEALTH PROBLEMS

Health problems, such as swollen tonsils, impacted anal glands or sore ears, will affect the dog's performance in the ring. It is amazing how many show dogs are not at their best because their owners have not been observant of their dog's well-being.

You have to constantly monitor your dog, be aware of its moods. If it is not eating, figure out why, don't just decide to stuff the dog without knowing if there is a medical problem. A dog that is not feeling well won't eat. Read your dog, and if you can't determine what is wrong, consult with your veterinarian.

If the dog has a weight problem, it either won't put on weight or will gain too much weight. It may be lethargic, won't grow good quality hair or may lack sex drive or overall energy. Your veterinarian should consider doing blood and enzyme screening tests.

Long-haired breeds take special grooming and preparation. This Shih Tzu is being readied for the ring.

The Terrier coat requires constant attention and a thorough knowledge of how to trim or hand strip. This is a Kerry Blue which requires careful scissoring.

This Irish Terrier is having its furnishings hand tidied.

18

Whatever the problem, the owner should be the first one to notice it. Often it is the professional handler who spots it when he or she takes a dog on to show.

HAIR AND COAT CONDITIONING

Water grows grass. Water grows hair. Clean hair grows. Dirty hair dies. There have been a lot of long-haired dogs in my kennel over the years, and they have grown a lot of coat. When dogs are being shown, they are bathed twice a week, once during the week and again the day before a show. There are a million different shampoos on the market and as many conditioners. But for routine bathing the shampoo should match the dog's natural pH content, which has a normal range of 5.5 to 7.2. The dog's skin is the most alkaline of all mammals, including humans.

Hair Preparations

Whether to use a conditioner, or which one, depends upon the breed. There are several other basics to remember:

- Some conditioners will soften the coat.

- Those that contain silicone will break the hair.

- Balsam has wax in it and may cause the skin to flake.

- It is not necessary to use the most expensive product on the market. Some of the best products can be bought at the local discount store.

You probably will have to experiment with various things to see which produces the right effect for your dog. Obviously this is not something you can do the night before a show. You have to try various things over a period of time to see what works best.

You may have to use different products at different times of the year, too, because when a dog is out of coat, you may want to use something to give the coat more body. Weather conditions are a factor, as well as whether shows are indoors or out. Dry heat in some buildings will necessitate a different conditioner, just as humidity in the summer will have an effect on the coat. The type of coat will determine the amount of conditioner you will use, and whether you will condition the whole coat or just the feathering. Most people use too much conditioner, which causes the coat to separate or to become oily.

Brushing

Daily brushing with a boar-bristle brush will stimulate the skin and enable hair to grow. This is effective for dogs with flat-lying, short to medium coats. However, a caution for those people with long-haired dogs and dogs with single silky coats. You must know how to brush the dog from the skin out without breaking the hair.

Grooming should be a relaxing and an enjoyable experience for both you and your dog. Coated show dogs spend a lot of time on the grooming table, so it should be pleasant time. No one wants to spend hours fighting with an unwilling dog on the table. Training a dog to enjoy the grooming process begins from the time the dog is old enough to stand up. Spend just a few moments a day in the beginning to accustom the dog to the height of the table and to being handled, stroked and brushed. Early conditioning will pay big dividends later on.

Hair grows from the inside out. Without proper nutrition, optimum health and exercise, a dog will never be in full bloom.

EXERCISE

A show dog has to be in great physical condition. Lying around on the couch all day isn't going to cut it. Good condition means as hard as a rock. Some dogs are that way naturally and some have to work at at. Dogs that are not normally active will need some help in the form of forced exercise. *But no dog should be given any involuntary exercise until it is two years of age or older.*

Puppies should be given the opportunity to play as much as they want, in areas big enough so that they get a chance to stretch their legs and run as hard and as fast as they want to, only as long as they feel like doing it.

Throwing a tennis ball or a Frisbee is fine as long as you quit when the dog starts to labor at it.

The Old English Sheepdog requires hours of brushing from the skin out to eliminate all tangles and mats.

The German Shepherd Dog with its flying trot must be conditioned daily. This dog gaits happily at a show.

No dog under the age of two should be jogged or exercised on a treadmill. With some breeds even two years is too young. All you will do is load up the shoulders and break down the pasterns.

Once you begin exercising the dog, whether jogging with you on a lead or putting it on a trotter, do it only until the dog begins to labor, then *quit*, whether it's a mile or 100 feet. When the dog is forced beyond its comfortable endurance, muscles that compensate will eventually turn into bad habits in movement. Your dog will take these learned negative patterns into the show ring and they will be practically impossible to break.

Build up the dog's endurance gradually so that it can do more and more, but *always* at its own pace. Walking is better exercise than galloping. If you are doing road work, either behind a car or on a machine, it should be done every other day. It takes twenty-four hours for those muscles that are basically injured to recuperate. Weight lifters do not do the same exercises every day. They alternate their routines so that their muscles have a chance to heal. If the dog exercises hard one day, it should rest by doing something different the next. If you use a jogger, blow a fan in front of the dog's face so that the dog thinks it is going someplace. It gives a little motivation. If left on their own, very few dogs will exercise. Most will sleep, or sit and watch the squirrels, but won't chase them.

All dogs need to be shown in hard flesh, even the Toy breeds. When the judge physically examines a dog he or she does not want to feel flab. A judge must feel that the dog is in firm condition. Proper exercise will stimulate the circulation as well as help hair growth. Therefore, you can see that everything that you do with your dog interacts with everything else.

FINDING YOUR DOG'S BUTTONS

From puppyhood on you should be observing your dog, finding out what makes it tick, trying out different things to see if the dog responds better to some than to others. That's called finding your dog's buttons. Some dogs like to be scratched behind the ears. If you want your dog to do something, give a little scratch and a little encouragement.

The career of one of the most famous Boxers of all time almost never got off the ground. He was an absolute deadhead, nothing interested him. His ears were down, his tail was down and he was just about to be shipped back to California by his handler, when by accident the handler found the dog's button. The handler's grandchild had left a small rubber ball lying in the yard, and the handler tripped over it. Being annoyed, he kicked the ball across the yard. The dog went out and hit the end of a six-foot lead, ears up, tail up, and he froze on that ball. From then on the rubber ball went to every show and the Boxer won 125 Bests in Show during his career.

The practice of free-baiting Labradors in this country came about when the handler of a great Labrador imported from England began to do it. Sam had a perfect front and loved treats, and would set himself up naturally, so to free-bait him made perfect sense. Pretty soon other handlers started baiting their dogs, despite the fact that their dogs might have looked terrible.

Years ago Collies were always shown hard-stacked, until one dog came along. He would look like a million bucks until you put your hands on him. Then the tail would go down and the ears would shoot out to the side like a bat. His handler was in despair and about to send him home until one day a man walked by the grooming table with a package in his hand. The dog came to life—tail out, ears up—and the handler went running down the aisle after the man to find out what he had in that bundle. This was in Canada, and the man had bought some moose meat. Well, you can bet the handler imported moose meat from that time on. That dog went on to become one of the most famous Collies in history.

Finding a dog's buttons may happen right away, or it may take months. Sometimes, as in the stories above, it happens by accident. Owner-handlers have the advantage here because they are with their dogs all the time and can experiment with different things.

There is usually a solution to almost any problem. For example, if a dog hates to have its mouth opened, you're in trouble in the show ring. You'll have to find a way to make that dog like to have its mouth examined. Maybe bait will work, maybe scratching under the chin. Ask other people to examine the dog's mouth. Then, praise or give a treat. This isn't going to happen overnight. It may take weeks of positive reinforcement to get that dog to like to have its mouth opened. But eventually, when the dog sees the judge coming closer, the dog will think there's going to be a reward, and your problem is solved.

If you run up against a stumbling block in training, or even

This Boxer is learning to bait.

This Shepherd free-baits on the way to winning Group 1.

A lady practices free-baiting her Petit Basset Griffon Vendeen before going into the ring.

when you're showing, don't be afraid to ask for advice, or even to pay for the solution. Good owner-handlers or professionals will help you if they can, provided you ask at the right time. Don't go up to handlers just as they are about to go into the ring. The only professionals that won't help you are those who don't have enough knowledge, and then they'll bypass the question.

   Training is indoctrination in the correct way to do things and is also the ability to do them the same way every time. *Teaching* is the means by which you motivate your dog to do what you want happily and consistently. To do both you have to read your dog and know your dog every day under every conceivable situation.

Gaiting a Golden Retriever requires good physical condition on the part of the handler as well as the dog.

3

Back to Basics

MOST OF THE INFORMATION in this book concentrates on the psychological aspects of showing a dog. However, without a thorough grounding in the fundamentals of physically showing a dog, none of the mental preparation will be useful. It is necessary to constantly refine and commit to memory those basic steps in stacking and gaiting a dog.

HUMAN CONDITIONING

It has to be recognized, too, that humans, frail creatures that we are, are prone to aches, pains and accidents that not only are uncomfortable to live with, but can seriously affect the way you show your dog. Knee injuries, back sprains and tendonitis are among the most common afflictions of the professional handler. The constant up and down motions of kneeling to stack a dog, running in circles on hard floors or bumpy grounds and standing around doing nothing for long periods of time take a toll on those who engage in this activity week in and week out.

You have to be in reasonably good physical condition to be able to show a dog well. Obviously, some breeds require a great

Stepping out with an Irish Setter requires timing, coordination and stamina.

A handler showing a Pekingese must bend and lift.

It is possible to compete successfully even though you cannot gait on two legs.

28

deal more fitness and stamina than others. When you see a German Shepherd Dog handler or an Afghan Hound exhibitor flying around the ring, you know that is not a breed for the fainthearted. However, even the Toy breeds require some bending and lifting and walking to show them properly.

You need to evaluate your own level of physical capability, and perhaps even go into training yourself before you can think of becoming a team with an active dog. Exercising with a dog is a good way to get in shape, in addition to using that time to practice gaiting your dog. Dogs have a rhythm to their gait, and when left on their own to trot, will fall into a natural rhythm that is comfortable for them. The secret to gaiting a dog so that it looks its best is to find a speed easy enough for both of you to accomplish so that you look like a team. This does not mean that you must adapt to the dog's pace, especially if your dog is lagging or does not look good, but you must find an accommodation that works for you as well as for the dog.

This takes practice that can be done at home, but also must be done under actual ring conditions. Practicing with mirrors or with someone watching you or videotaping is most valuable as you will have a critique of your performance to use as a learning tool.

ENTERING THE RING

Going into the ring is the obvious first step. But it is often right at that point that the amateur loses the class.

You must know ahead of time where you are going to stand and head there without stumbling over your feet or the dog. Once you arrive at your place in line, you have about ten seconds to set the dog up properly.

Most amateurs feel that they are not doing their job properly unless they are constantly fussing with the dog. If you watch an amateur, they are forever fixing one foot, moving another foot, changing the position of the lead, trying to perfect the stack, when in reality most of the time they are messing up the dog before the judge's eyes.

When you walk into the ring and gait around in the circle for the first time, leave enough room in front of you to slow down and walk your dog into a stack. When you come to a stop, there should be 3 feet between you and the dog in front of you. Before you begin fixing things, look at your dog. It may be that on its own the dog is in a position that is almost perfect. If so, don't fiddle. Only correct the feet that need correcting. You may only have to move one foot or two, or maybe none.

If you dash around the ring and come to an abrupt stop at your place, guaranteed you will have thrown your dog off balance and you will have to completely set all four feet. However, if you allow the dog leeway to comfortably walk into a stack most of the time, you will not need to constantly fuss with it. Your dog will look better, feel better, and you will be less flustered doing busy work.

LEADS ON, LEADS OFF

Some breeds, mostly Sporting dogs, are shown stacked with the leads off. However, sometimes the judge requests that you leave your lead on. You must listen to the judge's instructions and follow them. Setters and some Spaniels are shown to the judge with the leads off. Others, such as Pointers, Weimaraners and Brittanys have the option of being shown with the leads either on or off, depending on the preference of the handler. If you have a breed in which it is customary to remove the lead, you must practice doing this so that you are not fumbling around either taking it off or putting it on.

One of the things you will need to practice is the art of rolling up your lead in your hand. You should have control of it so it is not bunched up with loose folds hanging out of the bottom of your palm. This goes for all breeds with the exception of German Shepherd Dogs. Their particular fashion is to have a long length of loose lead dangling as they run.

You will control the speed of the dog and the position of the lead by the amount of lead that comes out of your hand. You may find it advantageous to use a short length for individual gaiting and a longer length for the go-around. Until you are very sure of exactly how your dog will react in every situation, don't attempt to gait with 6 feet of lead waving in the air. It may look very fancy for some handlers to do this with some breeds, but do not copy this *or any* method just because it looks good on someone else. As an amateur you are better off to stick to the basics while learning proper presentation.

This girl has her English Cocker stacked on the table for the judge's examination. Note that this exhibitor has chosen to leave the lead on.

Gaiting a Golden Retriever down and back at an indoor class. This handler is using a short length of lead for the individual gaiting.

This Irish Setter handler should have turned his back to the judge while grooming in the ring.

The best lead to have is one through which you will be able to have control of the head of your dog. Leads of leather, synthetics, chain or nylon come in all sizes, widths and strengths. You will have to experiment with various types of collars and leads to determine which is the best for you with a particular dog. Most professional handlers have a tack box full of leads, and they use specific leads depending upon the dog. Some dogs respond well to a choke chain. Others hate it and will fight the handler all the way. Some dogs dislike the sound that a choke chain makes around their ears, and they will shake their heads or fight to pull out of the noose.

Whatever lead you use, when you enter the ring and remove the lead, get your dog in a position that you think looks good. Do not remove the lead on the first stack (for those breeds shown without a lead) unless it appears that the judge is going to examine every dog *before* asking the class to circle. You can determine this ahead of time by watching the classes before yours, or the breed before yours, if you have the same judge.

If it looks as if the judge will be going down the line carefully looking at everyone, then remove your lead and place it on the ground near the dog's head where you can reach for it quickly. This obviously applies to those breeds shown with leads off. You must do this without letting go of the dog or losing control of the dog's head. It is not necessary to remove the lead for a puppy, regardless of the breed. Do not ever remove the lead until the dog is stacked to your satisfaction.

STACKING

The business of initially stacking your dog competently and quickly is a prime reason for not being first in line. Unless you have a seasoned show dog, or are a whiz at setting up a dog in ten seconds, don't fight to be the head of the class. Let someone else play that game so that you have a few additional seconds to set your dog up.

Once the judge has gone down the line and the class has gaited together, unless you are first in line, you will have time to relax your dog. You do not have to keep your dog stacked and on its toes the entire time you are in the ring, especially in large classes. In a small class you will obviously be showing your dog actively during whatever time you are in the ring.

A student learning to stack an English Springer Spaniel with the lead off, as George Alston, in the role of instructor, resets the dog's legs.

George Alston stacking a Boxer with the lead on.

If you decide to do some grooming on your dog, turn your back to the judge and brush with the dog out of sight. When the judge has examined and gaited two or three dogs in front of you, begin to bring up your dog's level of enthusiasm. We will discuss the importance of the dog's mental attitude later in the book, but for now you must prepare yourself for your dog to be individually examined and gaited.

When the judge motions the dog in front of you to begin its gaiting pattern, bring your dog out and stack it as perfectly as you can. Whether it is a breed that is examined on the table or on the ground, now is the time for you to position everything so that the judge sees your dog's attributes in the best possible manner.

Do not fuss with the dog once you have it set up. If the judge resets the back legs, leave them alone. Don't second-guess. What the judge sees and what you see from behind the dog are often very different. The most common mistake that amateurs make is to set the rear legs too far back, throwing the dog off balance. If the judge pulls the legs underneath the dog, that judge is doing you a favor, trying to make your dog look its best. If you undo what has been done, the judge may think you are a jerk and write you off. It is amazing how many exhibitors insult the judge by resetting a dog.

GAITING

After the judge has examined your dog, you will be expected to gait in a pattern that was established with all dogs before you. Unless you are first in line (there's that disadvantage again), you should have been observant and should know what pattern to follow. If the judge has stated that the dogs should gait in a triangle, don't take it upon yourself to change the routine. That throws off the judge's concentration and it makes you look stupid.

The individual gaiting exercise is probably the most important part of the examination. You must learn to run or walk in a straight line, with the arm that holds the lead in a steady position away from your body. You must practice detaching your wrist from the rest of your body so that your arm does not bounce up and down as you run. Every jerk of the lead travels right down to the dog's neck. Your dog will feel like a yo-yo and consequently will gait in a choppy and uneven manner.

You can practice rolling your lead and gaiting with a rock or any small object at the end of the lead. In this series of photos George Alston demonstrates. Here the lead is held correctly.

Do not hold your arm above your head.

Do not have the lead dangling out of your hand.

35

When you begin to gait, the lead remains perpendicular to your arm with the lead coming out of the bottom of your hand.

The lead remains perpendicular as you gather speed. The lead also remains steady and does not jiggle up and down.

If you had a dog at the end of the lead, you would turn your body slightly towards the dog, keeping your arm level.

This handler gaits her Irish Setter correctly.

36

You can practice running in a straight line with your arm held parallel to the ground. Instead of the dog at the end of the noose, tie on a pet rock. This might cause some raised eyebrows by the neighbors, but never mind. They think you are crazy for having show dogs anyway! You should be able to run without having the rock bouncing at the end of the lead. Once you can do this, you can try it with your dog, and you will notice the difference in both the dog's gait and yours.

BAITING

Your individual gaiting pattern has been completed, and now is the time to use whatever means you have to get your dog to look attentive and alert. You can bait a dog by showing it a piece of liver, sausage, a ball or whatever turns the dog on. Be careful about what you use, however. One lady baited her dog on clam dip because that is what it liked. All was well and good until one hot day she reached into her little bait pouch and the whole thing exploded all over her and the judge.

Do not feed the dog a mouthful of food just as the judge is starting to examine the head. Judges hate handlers who bait their dogs so that they are leaping or twirling around and the judge cannot see what she wants to see.

Don't try to fool the judge into ignoring your dog's bad front by constantly facing away from the judge. That will be the first thing any judge will look for. If your dog has a fault, don't keep going back to it. Just leave it alone and concentrate on showing the good parts of your dog.

Most important, do not get in the way of the judge seeing your dog. Always keep the dog between you and the judge. It is very irritating to a judge to have to peer around someone to find the dog.

MAKING THE CUT

Once you have been gaited and gone to the end of the line, depending upon the size of the class, you can either relax, or you must actively show your dog, keeping both of your spirits and

Free-baiting a Bullmastiff to accentuate the arch of the neck at the moment just before the judge makes a decision.

Judge examines a class of Rhodesian Ridgebacks. Note how the handlers are concentrating on head presentation as the judge comes down the line for one last look. These handlers are using a combination of stacking and baiting to create the best picture for the judge.

enthusiasms high. After every dog has been examined and gaited, the judge will begin the selection process. In a small class the dogs may be shuffled around, placed in line in the preferred order, or they may be left as they were examined.

In large classes judges have different methods of sorting. Some pull out the dogs they wish to consider further and excuse the rest from the ring. Some divide the class, putting the "keepers" in one spot and the others in another. It is often a guessing game as to which side is which. A few judges, to thoroughly confuse the exhibitor and the ringside, put their "keepers" in the middle of the line surrounded by the others. Some judges place the class first to last, no matter if there are fifty dogs in the class.

At all-breed shows judges are more likely to excuse dogs than at Specialties. They believe it is more courteous to the exhibitor at a Specialty show to keep everyone in the ring, even if it is obvious that a dog is no longer in contention.

If you are one of those held for further consideration, you should be actively showing, keeping your dog's interest high and attitude alert. If it is obvious that the judge does not like your dog, there is no reason to keep working at a high pitch. Save it for another day.

Remember, the judge points at the end of the class, not at the beginning. Everything you have worked for—stacking, gaiting, baiting, once, twice or three times—comes down to the final go-around. Although many judges have already made up their minds before they signal the class to gait one last time, in close competition it is often that last trip around the ring that makes the difference. At that point you and your dog have to do everything right.

There is another consideration, too. Suppose the dog that the judge has mentally chosen suddenly goes lame on the final turn. That opens up the door for anyone else to slip through. Sometimes a little turn of fate can make the difference between win and lose. If you are not ready, you lose!

WINNING THE POINTS

Assuming that you have won your class, you will be required to return to the ring to compete for Winners Dog or Winners Bitch. If you are in the Open class you will need to stay in the ring, so you will have no time to relax yourself or your dog. You can spend the couple of minutes while you wait for the other class winners to enter the ring to calm your dog, brush out the feathering or fluff up the top knot. If it is hot, you can allow your dog to lick a little ice or put alcohol on the pads of the feet. Open class animals lead the line so you should be prepared to stack quickly and handle your lead efficiently. Often a judge will not require the Open dog or bitch that has just been judged to gait again, so you can relax your dog while the judge reexamines the other animals.

At the last go-around you and your dog must be up and showing, despite the fact that the other dogs have had the advantage of resting. This system is hard on young puppies, so it is important for you to save some energy and enthusiasm for the important final minutes in competing for the points.

Some judges hardly ever consider anything but Open dogs or bitches for the points. Others enjoy finding a young newcomer to put up. Whatever class you are in, you must show to the best of your ability because you never know where your competition may be coming from.

A good example of that was a young Newfoundland being shown in American Bred. Because he was a good dog he kept winning. After a few shows he was moved to Open and he still won. The owner asked, ''Where's the competition?'' and the handler replied, ''*You* are the competition!'' Don't ever sell yourself or your dog short, no matter what class you enter!

BEST OF BREED

Should you be awarded Winners Dog or Winners Bitch, you are eligible to compete for Best of Breed competition and for Best of Winners. You will be required to go directly from the previous class into breed competition. Again you will have very little time to collect yourself and your dog, but the good news is that you will be at the end of the line. In a large class of Specials this can make a significant difference. If there are only one or two, you will have to be on your toes from the time you collected your Winners ribbon and placed yourself behind the Specials dogs and bitches. You will go through the exact same routine as you did for class judging, with the exception that the judge will usually not want to reexamine your dog. You may be asked to stand to one side, or your dog may get a cursory look, just to refresh the judge's memory.

Once the judge has made cuts from the Specials, you will be pulled up behind them. If the judge has decided to seriously consider your dog for Best of Breed, you will be placed at the head of the line, and for the first time that day your dog will lead in going around. Sometimes this is a frightening aspect for a young dog, and one over which you have little control.

Most dogs do not mind being in front as long as they are accustomed to having dogs follow them, and in the classes in all likelihood they will have had that experience. It is essential that your dog have confidence in you, so that when you take off at a good trot, your dog will be happy to move out with you. If it has been taught to pay attention to you, distractions from behind will not have an effect. In situations such as these, the type of training used in Obedience work can be very helpful.

The emphasis in Obedience is for the dog to pay absolute attention to the handler without being distracted by other dogs or ringside interference. You want your dog's attention focused on you, but not to the extent that the dog is constantly looking up at you and therefore gaiting off stride. There is a happy medium toward which you must work during you practice sessions at home. Here again, however, the finishing touches must be done in the ring under actual conditions.

IN THE GROUP

We'll assume that it has been your lucky day and you have won Best of Breed. You will accept the congratulations of your competitors gracefully and retire to rest your dog before it is time to go into the Group. You will find out from the show superintendent in what order Groups will be judged and at what time. If you are unfamiliar with the Group system you may ask a professional handler about how long it will take to judge all the Groups before yours. With this information you can determine how long it will take to prepare your dog for the ring.

You will need to exercise and groom your dog just as if you were going in to the ring for the first time that day. You will do all the preparations to yourself and to the dog. The dog will sense that work is not over and will become excited and interested just seeing Mom or Dad getting ready.

Dogs in the Groups are usually called into the ring according to size, with the exception of a few shows, such as Westminster, where place markers naming each breed determine where you are to stand. If you have a small dog, you will want to head for the rear of the line, allowing the bigger, faster dogs to go ahead of you. Among the bigger dogs there is an occasional jockeying for position, but tradition in each Group usually dictates that. For instance, usually the German Shepherd Dog leads the Herding Group, the Afghan Hound leads the Hound Group and the Irish Setter heads the Sporting Group, as these dogs move out with a longer stride than anyone else.

If you have a dog that you know has a tremendous reach, you may wish to be placed in front of someone with a dog that moves at a much slower pace. It is acceptable form to ask that exhibitor if you may go ahead. This is especially true if you get into a Best in Show lineup where you may be in competition with an Irish Wolfhound or a Chihuahua. Often the judge will sort out the order for you, putting the larger dogs at the head of the line and the smaller ones to the rear.

In Group competition you will go through all the motions that you do in a regular class—stacking, gaiting, individual examination and stacking and gaiting for one final time. Judges in this class do not usually give exhibitors the benefit of a poor performance. Your practice of the basics will pay off for you here. You absolutely must know the fundamentals of stacking and gaiting because *winning in the Group and Best in Show rings is 90 percent mental.* If those routines have not made their own pathways in your brain, you are at a real disadvantage when you come up against the professionals who have been in this sport for their whole lives.

4

Obedience and Conformation

MANY PEOPLE wonder whether training a dog for Obedience will ruin it for the show ring. Not too many people worry about the opposite—will showing a dog in conformation destroy its attitude in the Obedience ring?

Actually, an Obedience trained dog can do very well in the show ring, and a ring-wise show dog can transfer those qualities of showmanship and attitude to the Obedience ring. In order to do both at the same time and do them well, the owner handler has to have very clear definitions of the goals of Obedience and conformation and tailor training methods for both.

It is most important for the dog to understand that the two activities are separate and therefore training techniques for each must be different and done at different times.

TRAINING FOR OBEDIENCE

The whole atmosphere of training for Obedience should be given its special place and time. Use a collar and lead which is only

Ch. Royal Tudor's Wild as the Wind, CDX won Best in Show at the Westminster K.C. show in 1989. In the same year she was Best of Breed at the Doberman Pinscher Club of America National Specialty.

Ch. Acadia Command Performance, CD won Best in Show at Westminster in 1973, after which he went on to earn a CDX degree.

taken out when the dog is training for Obedience. There are basic commands in Obedience, some of which are useful in the show ring and others which are never used. The dog must learn to distinguish among them, and by clearly defining when commands are used, the dog will learn fairly readily which is which.

The basic commands in Obedience are: Come, Heel, Sit, Down, Stay, Stand. The two most useful for the show dog are obviously Stay and Stand. These can be most effective in training the dog to stack without moving. The Obedience exercise Stand for Examination when done in the show ring can allow you to stack the dog, take your hands off, move back and let the dog stand out by itself for the judge to see. It is a most effective grandstanding play to see a perfectly still dog whose only movement is to acknowledge the judge's approach with its head.

At a recent Westminster show a Viszla in the Sporting Group had the crowds in the stands cheering wildly as it stacked itself to perfection and did not move a muscle except to turn its head towards the judge. The English Foxhound, Winslow, stacked himself and stood motionless, a technique he learned over the course of many months, but with no formal Obedience training.

The biggest problems exhibitors have with Obedience trained dogs are in gaiting. If they have not been taught to distinguish one ring from another they will do what they have been drilled to do for Obedience. They will hang beside the handler's knee, because in heeling for Obedience that is where they are taught to gait. There are some Obedience trainers who teach their students to have the dogs looking up at them the entire time they are gaiting, with the result that, not only are the dogs hugging the handler's leg, but they are twisting themselves into a pretzel looking up and sideways. This can cause problems in Obedience such as the dog bumping or heeling wide. Obviously, this will not do in the show ring, but if you train by this method the dog will get into bad gaiting habits which are difficult to break.

The other major gaiting problem is that Obedience dogs are taught to sit automatically when the handler stops, so that when you are at the end of your individual pattern the dog approaches the judge and sits. This can be overcome by instructing the dog to stand as you come up to the judge.

OBEDIENCE CLASSES

Almost all competitors attend some kind of training classes to prepare for Obedience Trials. There are as many Obedience training techniques as there are dogs to train, and the owner handler has to be particularly careful about the type of training the dog is subjected to. There are professional trainers, Obedience clubs which offer classes led by club members, and every one touts a particular philosophy of training.

Obedience training has progressed and branched out into a thousand methods since it first began in the 1930s. There are more books written about ways to train your dog than there are about raising a baby. Some of them are excellent, some are terrible, some are plain ridiculous and others contain good sections and bad. It is up to the owner to try to make some sense of all the information that is thrown at you. With Obedience training your own common sense about what is best for your dog is essential.

When you go to select an Obedience school or trainer, tell the instructor what your interest is—that you plan to show this dog at the same time that it is being trained to be a good canine citizen. It is important, especially during this period when the general public seems to be down on dogs, that your dog behaves in public, is responsive to commands and knows how to act around other people and dogs. For those reasons, if nothing else, *basic Obedience is a plus for any dog*. If you have a big dog, early Obedience training will make it much easier to handle that dog both in the show ring and the Obedience ring when it grows up.

When you decide to attend an Obedience class, go to a couple of sessions and watch how the instructor handles the dogs. You do not want anyone teaching your dog who believes in punishment methods of training. You want someone with soft hands who will *teach you* how to handle your dog properly. Often classes begin a session with an orientation in which the instructor explains his or her philosophy of training and sometimes demonstrates with their own dogs. It is very useful to attend one of these opening classes because you will get a good idea of how the instructor thinks. At the same time you can discuss your own goals for your dog.

You might decide that initially you do not want the dog to sit at the end of every heeling exercise. The instructor should be willing to make that allowance for you. Also, if you have a trainer that believes in the "pretzel" method of heeling, he or she should be willing to let you heel your dog in a more natural manner. If one instructor will not cooperate with you, find another, even if it means traveling some distance to get what you want. It will be well worth it in the end.

Unless you have a dog that is a real terror in the house, classes are better for the show dog than individual training sessions. This is because while you are teaching your dogs the commands, you are both getting ring experience leading and following other dogs. It will also be getting experience standing and waiting while others do their routines. A lot of time in the show ring is spent standing around and your dog has to become accustomed to this. An Obedience class where dogs are taught to be under control in the presence of other dogs and people is a good training ground for this.

Heeling

Once you have found your class and have enrolled your dog for the eight or ten week course, you will find that a lot of time is spent heeling. You will also spend your practice sessions at home heeling around the house, around the yard, around the neighborhood. While you are practicing this routine, be certain that your dog is gaiting in a straight line, just as you would be expected to do in the show ring. You should not gait your dog so close to your left side that it looks like it is attached to your leg. Gait it at a reasonable distance from you so that it can see you and respond to your commands, both verbal and body language, without turning towards you. Dogs have good peripheral vision so there is no need for them to be constantly looking up or twisting around to see you. When you come to a halt, do not go from a flat-out run to a stop so that the dog goes skidding into the judge or into a sit. Slow your pace over three or four steps so that when you stop the dog is standing by your side. At this point you can tell your dog to "Stand" and move a step away, or you can tell it to "Stand" and stand by its side.

During the Obedience training process you should always use the same collar and lead that you will use in the Obedience ring. You will do the same for your show training process. Always use the show lead that is associated with the show ring.

As you progress with your heeling pattern you can experiment by seeing if the dog responds appropriately to sitting in the Obedience sessions and standing in the show training sessions. Different

This handler uses body language, bait and a command to Stay as she comes back to the judge following the individual gaiting pattern.

This Malamute has been taught to Stand and Stay while waiting for the judge's examination. Except for the length of lead, this exercise is not unlike that used in the Pre-Novice Class.

equipment, different commands, and different body language on your part can help here. Often dogs are smart enough to tell the difference, but if your dog seems to be confused about what is expected, don't take the chance of having it automatically sit every time you stop. If you find this is happening as you come to a halt at the end of your gaiting pattern, tell the dog to "Stand."

As you are heeling you will learn how to get your dog to execute about-turns, both to the right and to the left. This is a very useful maneuver, for as you come to the end of the ring you will obviously have to go the other way. This is especially useful when you are executing the "L" pattern in which you are asked to go down to the end of the ring, across and back and return to the judge. How many times have you seen exhibitors fumbling with the lead, tripping over the dog, whirling around in circles as they try to turn and go the other way.

In Obedience class the dog will learn how to turn into the handler, away from the handler or to follow around the handler without losing control. This can all be done by hand motions without commands, or the dog can be taught to "turn" on command in the direction that the handler indicates by the use of the lead.

Stand for Examination

The other important Obedience command which is very useful is the "Stand and Stay." As we just described, you can walk your dog into the "Stand" at the end of the gaiting pattern, and you can teach it to stand on the stack. At the beginning every time you stack your dog, give the command to "Stay" and praise the dog for a correct response. In Obedience class you will not be asked to stack your dogs, but you will be told to "stand for examination." Your instructor should be willing to allow you to stack your dog in a show pose. For those breeds who are normally free-stacked and baited, this exercise is a natural. The dog will learn that both in the show ring and in the Obedience ring the judge will come to examine the dog, walk around and stare and the dog must stand still.

Other Obedience Commands

The commands "Down" and "Come" should pose no conflict at all in the show ring, and, in fact, can be a great advantage in terms of control and safety, anywhere you take your dog. Since exhibitors spend a great deal of time, especially in large classes, waiting for their turn, it is useful to be able to tell a dog to lie down in order to be quiet and rested beforehand. By doing this the dog is out of the sight of the judge while being brushed or not looking its best, is not getting into trouble with other dogs in and outside of the ring, and in hot weather is staying calm and cool. The handler is not becoming frustrated, hot and bothered by having an uncontrollable dog at the end of the lead.

The other advantage to having a dog lie down and stay down on command is during the grooming process. Most coated breeds, especially those needing hours of attention, are taught at an early age to lie down and stay in one position on the grooming table. Transferring this to the Obedience ring should be easy.

How many times have you seen a dog bounding gaily through several rings, having a wonderful time greeting spectators at ringside and other dogs as it whisks by at top speed? Fellow exhibitors and the gallery grasp for it in vain as it skitters out of reach. If that dog had been taught to "Come" on command, it might have a little tour around the neighboring rings, but it would return to its owner as it was trained to do.

Teaching a dog to come when called is the most difficult exercise of all. Any dog will respond almost instantly while it is on the end of a lead, but once that restraint is gone, it is a far different matter and one which is beyond the scope of this book. However, rest assured, all the trouble, heartache, and especially patience, it takes to teach this command can make the difference between a trained dog and companion and an outlaw or a dead dog. Teaching a dog to come under all conditions can also save its life by preventing it from running into the street or off the show grounds into traffic. Obedience classes can make a start on this, and under controlled situations, such as an Obedience ring, the dog will obey, but teaching the "come" under all conditions takes infinitely more of everything.

Retrieving

The other useful command for the show ring occurs when the dog is advanced in Obedience and is taught to retrieve. Retrieving should ideally be taught to a very young puppy, because the instinct to play, carry toys and be close to the owner is strongest then. Any dog can be taught to find an object and to bring it back. It is a universal game which most dogs seem to play instinctively.

Once you have taught the dog whatever words you want to use for this game, whether it be "look," "find," "get it," "fetch" or "bring it," you can carry this over both to the Obedience and show ring. In Obedience, the object is to find an object and bring it back to the handler. In the show ring, you want the dog to look for something ahead of it, so that the dog will be out in front of you, alert, with attention focussed on the surroundings. A dog who is interested in looking at things in and out of the show ring will be a better show dog. This is because it has a lively curiosity and therefore shows more personality in the ring.

As an example of this, a Gordon Setter in the Group ring suddenly spotted a bird outside the ring and went on a solid point. The judge said, "I can't deny that," and gave the dog first place.

Puppies who spy a butterfly and hold themselves three inches taller on their toes present a winning picture. A handler can mimic those conditions by encouraging the dog to "look" or "find" and because of the happy associations of playtime with those words, the dog presents a better picture in the show ring.

A CAUTION

The biggest problem with Obedience training a show dog comes, not with the dog, but with the handler. It cannot be stressed too emphatically that harsh training methods of any kind will be totally counterproductive. You will have a dog that drags around the ring, lagging behind the owner, timid and afraid to assert itself. This may be true in the Obedience ring also, but while a dog that performs all the exercises without error but without enthusiasm may still qualify, that will not be enough to win in *either* ring.

Obedience training can be of great benefit, certainly in producing a better companion, and in the show ring if used with discretion and common sense.

It took many months of training to get this English Foxhound to show like this.

5

Training for
the Show Ring

WHAT IS the first thing you do in preparing a dog for the show ring?

You train. How many times have you been to a show and heard someone say, "This dog had a lead on for the first time ten minutes ago." They think that's clever. Of course, when they walk into the ring, it looks like it. Why would anyone want to waste an entry fee taking a bucking, balking puppy into the show ring?

More good show dogs are ruined because the initial training is not done properly than any other one thing. It's great for the professionals' bankbook, because they get to show all the dogs that the owners can't do anything with after they've destroyed them.

TRAINING FOR TWO

Training comes in two parts, training your dog and training yourself. You can train a dog no matter what age, whether it is a young puppy or four or five years of age. Show training is a process, just like training for Obedience, finding people, Tracking or whatever. You use a series of rewards and nonrewards. The least amount of negative reinforcement, the better. There may be times you will have to use negative reinforcement, but it should be used *only* for the most serious occasions.

If you use a little common sense in your training process, you will get better results.

At no time should you ever use food for motivation. The dog should show for love, which is a lot stronger motivation than a piece of liver.

Ideally, initial training should be done between six and twelve weeks. *Absolutely no training should be done during the teething process*, usually between twelve weeks and six to nine months, depending upon the breed. You can walk the puppy around on a loose lead, but that's all. The reason that you do not want to apply lead pressure, or any forcible training, is that when dogs are teething, they have no attention span. There is no consistency in their reactions from one day to another. Their resistance is down, their tonsils are enlarged, their glands are enlarged, their teeth hurt, their mouths hurt and they hate it. Remember, the whole idea in training for the show ring is to make it fun for the dogs.

Training involves not only the actual working with the dog, stacking or gaiting, but also learning about your dog. Just like when you live with a person you learn their likes and dislikes, what turns them on and what turns them off, you have to use this information to get the response you want from your dog.

You don't want the dog to associate showing with training, and that is one reason why dragging a puppy around the ring the first time it has a show lead around its neck can ruin it.

Training sessions should be kept short. Never more than ten minutes at a time. You can train in two short sessions during the day, but in the real-life show ring you will never have to physically show your dog longer than ten minutes in any one competition. Guaranteed. If you spend more than ten minutes training, you are doing it wrong. You are not relaxing either yourself or the dog.

Showing basically is comprised of two elements: gaiting and stacking. These two things should be taught separately. You can teach a dog to gait on a lead in five minutes. You can teach a dog to stack in two minutes, but the hardest thing for the dog to understand is the transition from stack to gait. Do not combine the two until the dog understands each one thoroughly.

STACK TRAINING

In stack training you are teaching the dog to accept your hands on its body, that you are going to take the dog's legs and "twist them around and put them in unnatural places." Your dog has to learn that you will hold its head in an awkward position and that the dog will learn to like this. You will go through these exercises, and if the dog accepts them and does them correctly, you will give lots of praise. If the dog does not do it, you are not going to say anything. You will just ignore the reactions and do it again. After a while the dog will understand that if the exercise is done right, there will be praise and love. If it is done wrong, the dog will be ignored. This method takes a little longer, but you will have a dog that will show better over an entire career. Basic training is the beginning of a show dog's career and should be enjoyed.

Ideally you should begin getting a puppy accustomed to being handled and put into a show (stack) position before twelve weeks of age. Puppies learn quickly between the ages of eight and twelve weeks. A few minutes a day on the grooming table and on the ground at this young age will be remembered when the dog is older.

The dog must accept having its head held and its teeth examined. This can be practiced alone and then with someone else going over the head and looking into the mouth. If the dog objects, don't fight with it. Release your grip so that only your fingers are holding the muzzle. Give the other person some bait to use so that the dog associates having its head touched with a reward, given after the examination is complete.

Practice stacking in front of a mirror, so you can see how the dog looks.

The dog must be stacked in such a way that you are comfortable. If you are 5 feet 2 inches and weigh ninety pounds you will not be able to arm wrestle a Mastiff into a decent stack. You will have to train the dog to stack itself with its four feet where you want them to be. You can walk a dog into a perfect stack, but *the mistake that most handlers make is to constantly rearrange the dog when they should be leaving it alone.*

A dog who constantly fidgets, moving one foot and then the other, needs a firm grip on the head. Once the head is in position, the dog will be off balance if it moves. Since this is not comfortable

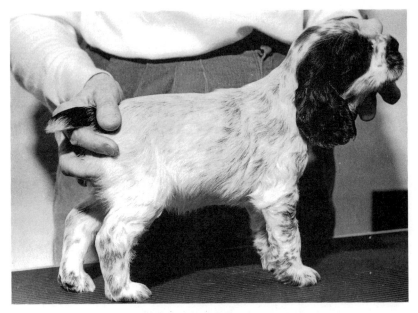

Stack training an English Cocker puppy on the table at six weeks.

Stacking an Irish Setter outdoors while training, allows the dog to feel less crowded and more at ease.

for the dog, it will eventually get the idea that it is better to stand still.

When you are stacking a dog, always keep control of the head, either with your hand under the jaw or with a lead up under the ears. Do not relax the head while you are adjusting the feet, or the dog will move away from you and you will have to begin all over again.

You will have to find which technique is best for you. Small dogs are easily stacked either on the table or on the ground, but the same principles apply. Stacking a large dog requires more physical effort and coordination. You will have to choose the method that is best for you.

Once you have decided on the quickest, most efficient method of getting your dog's head positioned correctly, four feet pointing in the same direction (usually straight ahead) and the tail held where it is supposed to be, then stay with the method you have chosen.

The dog will learn what you want much faster if you are completely consistent in where and how you put your hands on its body.

Practice stacking with a minimum of motion. You should be able to stack a dog in three minutes, once you have figured out in your own mind the simplest way for you to get your dog looking good.

GAIT TRAINING

A puppy should be taught to walk on a loose lead in the same time frame, though not in the same lesson, as it is taught to stack. This should occur before twelve weeks of age.

There are different methods of teaching a dog to accept a loose lead. Some people put a light buckle collar on the puppy and leave it until it stops leaping, throwing itself around and trying to scratch it off. Once it realizes that the collar isn't such a torment, you may attach a lead to the collar and follow the puppy around as it runs from place to place.

After your dog has learned to accept this thing that connects it to you, you can coax, cajole and make a game of having the puppy follow you. There should be no harsh jerks or corrections using the lead at this time nor when the dog is older and ready to be "lead broken" to a show lead.

After the puppy is through the teething process you can teach it to gait on a show lead, using a series of small jerks to bring it along in the direction you want to go at the pace you set.

Initial gait training should always be done on a loose lead. Absolutely, positively! It does not matter what breed it is. At no time should you use any constant steady pressure on the lead. It should always be a series of small corrections. Gradually increase those corrections just to the point that the dog responds properly. You will find after a while that your corrections become fewer and fewer, so that you believe the dog can almost read your mind.

Occasionally you may have to give a sharp correction with the lead if the dog is forging out of control, but you should try to keep these corrections to a minimum. Never jerk a dog that is lagging, or it will hang back even farther. Encourage a lagger by talking and showing a piece of bait. You will have better results controlling a dog just learning to gait if you keep the lead fairly short and your arm steady. If the dog is bouncing all over the place and hits the end of the lead that you are holding just over its head at the end of your steady arm, it will correct itself without your having to say or do anything.

When you see a dog in the ring with a top professional, it will look like the handler is not doing anything, or just waving the lead slightly. That dog is responding to the initial training process of correction and release, pull and release. As the dog learns to respond, the handler has to do less of this.

FUNDAMENTALS

These are the fundamentals. Too many people try the fancy stuff without learning the basics. When any coach or manager of any sport is asked to define the secret of their team's success, or any individual player in a sport such as golf or tennis is asked how they turned around from mediocrity to success, almost to a person the answer involves going back to basics. They have to learn and relearn the fundamentals of that sport so they do not have to think about them.

The same rules apply to showing dogs. You must know the fundamentals of stacking and gaiting by heart so that you do not have to concentrate on them. Even after you have learned these basics you will find the need during the dog's show career to go back and reinforce them, both to correct bad habits and to practice so they remain second nature.

If the basic mechanics are not learned by the exhibitor to perfection, some of the techniques in this book will be totally useless. They should be learned so that most mental concentration can be spent on the presentation of the dog.

DOGS SHOWS ARE FUN

Dog shows must be fun for the dog. How many people have dogs that hide the moment the show lead comes out? It should be the other way around. You have to teach them to like the ring. If you do not do this basic thing, you will not have a show dog and you will not do any winning in the Group and Best in Show competition. When it gets down to the end and all the dogs in the ring are worthy, it is the personality and showmanship of the dog that is going to make the difference.

Most handlers would tell you that they would rather have a good show dog than a good dog any day. That is for two reasons. When you get beaten showing a good dog, it is a real big downer. When you win with an average dog that is a good show dog, even though it isn't a top specimen of the breed, it makes the handler feel good because it means he or she was able to use talent to bring out the best in that dog.

You should want your dog to drag you to the ring and not away from it. Most owner-handlers and inexperienced professionals have dogs that show better going away from the ring than going to it or being in the ring. It's all because of training and how the dog is taught. Watch the dogs in Group and Best in Show competition. The top winners are happy, but they weren't born that way. It's like acquiring a taste for clams or oysters. Can you imagine the first man or woman who ever opened up an oyster and ate it raw? Now that was a person with character! Think of the first time you ever tried a clam or an oyster. You had to acquire the taste, and some of us never have. If you make showing fun for the dog, you will have the fun and satisfaction of showing a winner.

A Wire Fox Terrier learning that shows are fun. This is something that is essential for *any* show dog.

It will take a lot of motivation to convince this Irish Setter that it's more fun to show.

TRANSITION FROM STACKING TO GAITING

Once the dog has learned to stack and to gait during separate training sessions over a period of two to four weeks, then you can slowly bring the two sessons closer together, making the transition time shorter. Eventually the dog will be able to go from a stack position and remaining very, very still, to the gaiting and moving with direction and enthusiasm.

From this point on, after the dog has learned both and is doing them well, all training and refining of these actions should be done in the ring.

BAIT: USE IT AS A TOOL

One additional point. During the initial training process, no food or baiting should be done for any breed, even if it is a breed that is normally free-baited. Owner-handlers of breeds such as Collies, Shelties, Min Pins, Keeshonds and others, with the exception of Doberman Pinschers, make the mistake of only free-baiting their dogs. Then, when at some point they have to set their dogs up, the dog rebels. Baiting is the last thing that the dog should be taught, only after the dog knows the basics.

Bait should be used as a tool to bring the most out of a dog. It should be used to gain attention, get the ears up, brighten the sparkle in the eye, give a proper arch to the neck. The ideal is to use bait as an enhancer, but not as an all-encompassing function, neglecting the other aspects of training and showing a dog.

HOUSE DOGS/KENNEL DOGS

It is much more difficult to train a house dog to be happy in the ring than a kennel dog, but it can be done. Dogs primarily want you to approve of what they do. They want your friendship.

If you have a dog that is not showing well for you, ignore the dog. Regardless of whether it is in a kennel situation or a home situation, leave the dog alone. Don't discuss the daily news with your dog. Don't sit on the couch and pat your dog. Don't even let the dog know where the food comes from. Ignore the dog except

English Springers are usually shown stacked in the ring and then must turn on the charm when gaiting.

Stacking and teaching a Newfoundland to bait to show expression.

when the lead is on. Take the lead out, put it on—fun and games. Take it off, ignore the dog. Within one week your dog will do flips when that lead is brought out.

BUILD GRADUALLY

Too many owners take a dog into the ring for the first time, especially a six-month-old puppy, and they want the dog to perform like a veteran show dog. They get upset and forget that it took a professional a year or two years to get that dog to perform in that manner. Forget about winning or losing the first four to six times in the ring. Go into the ring to make it fun for the dog. Bring out the ball, the liver, the treats. Pet and play with your dog in the ring.

The training should be a slow, building process. Young puppies are not perfect. Kids are not perfect. A sixteen-year-old youth is not expected to have the social graces of a forty-five-year-old man or woman who has been through life.

Just as people change, dogs change. As the dogs mature mentally and physically, so your training process is an ever-changing thing. You will find that as dogs develop, they are able to do things that they cannot do at a younger age. The converse is equally true. You have to adjust and adapt to the dog's mental and physical capabilities at each stage of its life.

There may be a certain aspect of showing that the dog cannot comprehend at six months of age. Just because the dog cannot do it then, don't throw it away. Go back and try it at a later date if you feel that a particular thing is going to help your dog's presentation.

As an example, your dog may not be able to gait fast at ten months of age because of being physically incapable of doing it. Developing muscles and coordination don't allow for it. It's like a thirteen-year-old kid who's trying to be a ballet dancer. At two and a half years of age, after your dog's muscles and mind mature, you will be able to increase the dog's gaiting speed.

During the dog's entire show career, you should be looking for things to improve—both the handler's presentation and the dog's presentation. Just because a dog looks good at two years of age showing a certain way does not mean that will be the best way to show the dog at three or four.

PRACTICING CORRECTLY

Practicing or refining either the dog's abilities or the handler's abilities are generally done incorrectly by the amateur. To put this in perspective, professional athletes, either in golf, football, baseball, basketball or any other team or individual sport, practice things that they don't do well. Most amateurs practice what they do well. This is wrong.

Practice should be used to get rid of bad habits and increase physical or mental ability. If you do something excellently, why practice it? When you practice at home with your dog, concentrate on the aspect with which you are having problems, such as stacking, setting the legs quickly and correctly, showing the bite, getting the dog to move fast or move slow.

Most amateurs have difficulty moving in a straight line. As they weave down the ring, the dog is thrown off balance. Practice a simple routine such as running along a fence, or marking off a line with string so that your dog moves correctly. You might choose a spot or object in your sight line and move toward that as you gait your dog.

Most people go out to practice, and if the dog is having trouble stacking but gaits well, they spend the whole session gaiting, or vice versa.

You should get a large mirror so that you can see what your dog looks like when it is set up. What the dog looks like to the judge is completely different from your view behind the dog. You have to learn what your dog looks like to you and how it appears to the judge. When you have your dog stacked, it may feel and look terrible to you, but from the judge's point of view it may look gorgeous. The opposite may be true, also. If you are behind your dog and everything looks perfect to you with all parts fitting together, from the judge's viewpoint 30 feet away the dog may look ugly as sin.

The Blind Side

Another way for you to practice your skills is to set your dog up with a blindfold. Stand there and ask someone to tell you what looks correct and what looks incorrect, so that eventually you will be able to set your dog up almost without looking. After you have practiced blindfolded, you will be able to do it with only a small

Gaiting a Petit Basset Griffon Vendeen may require adjusting the stride of both dog and handler. Particularly with short-legged dogs, the handler must learn to take cues from the lead to know what the dog is doing.

This German Shepherd Dog finds a reward after winning the Group and enjoys some positive reinforcement while in the ring.

part of your vision so that you can keep your eyes on what else is going on in the ring.

A dog cannot move without shifting its weight. By using a blindfold you can teach your hands to feel weight shift from one leg to another. This technique becomes very useful when the judge suddenly looks at you. If you have felt the dog move, you can compensate immediately, before the judge sees it. This takes practice and finesse, something the professional has already learned, whether on purpose or by accident.

You also have to learn that your dog's movements and interaction with the lead should be giving you a clue as to what your dog is feeling and what is going on with dog mentally, whether the two of you are fighting or are a team. You have to adjust this pressure and your actions to achieve the proper performance.

In the end, in the last show of a career, you should try to achieve your dog's most perfect performance. The two of you should be reading each other's minds, so that it looks as if you and the dog can be doing this without any lead contact at all.

POSITIVE REINFORCEMENT

How many people have had an animal that has been unsure, so that the dog goes into the ring tail down, no spirit, pulling to get back to the car to go home. Most people will stand outside the ring and play with the dog, give a treat, show the ball. Then when the time comes to go into the ring, they force the dog to stand. Gone are the ball and the treats. The dog thinks, "Outside the ring we play, inside the ring I get discipline. I don't like this a bit."

There are other ways to practice positive or passive reinforcement while you are training for the show ring. If you have a shy dog, do not pat it or say, "That's OK" By doing that you are reinforcing the shy behavior. Instead, ignore the dog. Don't do anything, but when you get into the ring, play with your dog so that you help to build confidence.

Handling classes are for training you, not the dog. If you go for the dog's benefit, forget it. You'd do better for the dog by going down to the park to the local softball game. Meet people. Hang out, be cool! But do not use classes as a means of socializing the dog.

Classes are stressful for a dog, and you are taking that dog and trying to train under stress conditions. *No training should be done under stress.* Absolutely, positively! All this does is make the dog hate the activity. You have to teach your dog to love show training. No one, not human or dog, can learn well and learn to enjoy when the stakes are high during the learning process.

At some point Little League games will not suffice. Dogs will have to be introduced to other dogs. It's better to go to a match than to handling classes. Matches are less stressful because dogs are not in the ring for a long period of time. In handling class you are in the ring for an hour or two at a stretch. Instead, go to the match and let your dog play and have fun. If you win, fine; if you don't, fine! Your goal is not for a win in a puppy class at a match show. Your goal is for a superb showdog at the prime of a future career.

Training each breed is different. For instance, English, Irish and Gordon Setters are each completely different in temperament. Gordon Setters do not mature mentally or physically until they are about four or five years old. English Setters mature earlier, but have about ten shows in them before they quit. Irish Setters just like to show off.

Some people once had an English Setter that they called Fat Albert. He hated dog shows, but he loved to sit on the couch and eat sausage biscuits for breakfast. When he came to our kennel, he didn't get his sausage biscuit in the morning. He got it in the ring. Pretty soon he was dragging me to the ring so that he would get the sausage biscuit his mother always provided for him.

There was an English Foxhound that was brought to me to show when he was four and a half years old. He had never had a lead on, and had lived his whole life in a pack, where he hunted foxes. The minute the lead went around his neck, all four feet went into the air and he was upside down on the ground. After about a month of seeing him with all his feet in the air, I drove up to watch the huntsman train hounds. I thought I was a good dog man until I watched that master stand forty dogs in a row without raising his voice or using his hands. I learned that Foxhounds are contrary, so every time I wanted that dog to do something, I did the opposite. He turned out to be one of the greatest show dogs ever in my kennel, but it took nine months to train him after I learned how to get into a Foxhound's head.

THIS IS ENTERTAINMENT

It can't be emphasized too often that the dog must enjoy what it is doing in order to be a top show dog. A show dog's entertainment is in the ring. This is opposed to a dog whose recreation and playtime are retrieving a ball, playing with a Frisbee or working in the field. A dog has to think shows are more fun than sitting on the couch, drinking a beer and watching the ball game.

If your dogs are having a lot of fun, you will have dogs that will respond to you until the last time they ever walk into the ring. There have been dogs that walked into Veterans classes at ten, twelve or thirteen years of age more enthusiastic than they were at the prime of their careers. Ideally, you want your dogs to scream if left at home because they know you are going to a show without them.

STARTING SLOWLY

Make your dog's first contact with shows enjoyable. Don't start a dog off by going to a two- or three-show weekend for several weekends in a row. If you go to a three-show weekend, show your dog the first day, don't show the second day and then show the third day. Your dog should still go to the middle show. Go through all the motions except the grooming and showing of the dog.

Then skip a weekend and don't go. If you're going anyway, leave the dog home. When the other dogs return, they'll let Star know they were at a dog show and they had fun. Then Star will want to go the next time.

Don't show a young dog straight down the line. For the first six months of a dog's career it might be shown twelve to fifteen times, and gradually increased as you see how the dog likes it and what progress the dog makes.

Do not start a dog off on a career with a stressful long circuit or at a particularly stressful large show. It is better to go to small shows, where you have the time and are not rushed and conditions are pleasant.

Absolutely, positively do not start a dog off on a show career in hot weather. If you are taking a dog to a show for the first time, and on the way you hear that the temperature is going to be 110 degrees, turn around and go home. Forget the almighty ribbon and think of the dog.

Make your dog's first contact with shows enjoyable.

During your training sessions you are finding out what things your dog responds to and what things will not work with that dog. These buttons may not always work the same under different show conditions. What was exciting, relaxing or interesting at home under normal living circumstances may not be the same under stress conditions. A dog in the living room might like a good back scratch and become very laid-back and mellow. However, in the show ring if you do the same thing, the dog may become totally wired.

You will only find out what works by getting into the ring and experimenting with your dog. That is the reason why basic training must be done at home, but all finishing work has to be done under actual ring conditions.

This handler takes a moment to convince his charge that he is the best dog in the ring.

6

The Psychology
of the Show Ring

THE SPORT OF DOGS is 80 percent mental and 20 percent physical. You can beat yourself mentally before you ever step into a show ring.

In the past ten years there has been a lot of information gathered about the use of psychology in sports. Football teams have their own sports psychologists who are supposed to motivate the players into a winning attitude. They are encouraged to fight against pain, to overcome whatever physical obstacles they encounter through mental preparation. Basically, the whole concept is to have a positive outlook, to think that your team is going to win and that you are going to play the best game of your life.

There have been important controlled studies of athletes who have prepared themselves intellectually as well as physically compared to those whose knowledge of their sport was limited. Those who were mentally prepared for the demands of competition performed significantly better than athletes who did not receive such training.

Studies described in books published as early as 1970 gave

examples of athletes who rigorously learned their sport, concentrating as much on the mental preparation as on physical prowess. Three books on the subject showed the importance of the mind in preparing an athlete for competition. These were *Psychological Preparation of the Elite Athlete* and *Psychological Preparation and Athletic Excellence*, both by Bryant Cratty (Movement Press) and *Psychology and the Superior Athlete* by Miraslaw Vanek and Bryant Cratty (Macmillan). These are no longer in print but may be available through libraries.

Another book, *Psychocybernetics*, by Dr. M. A. Maltz (Simon and Schuster), first published in 1960, describes the effects of mind over matter. In studies conducted on several hundred people, those who practiced a skill mentally, such as throwing darts without ever lifting a dart, threw more accurately than those who practiced throwing darts physically but without mental preparation. Those who both practiced and engaged in mental preparation for about thirty minutes a day came out best.

THE POWER OF THE MIND

The power of the mind is as important when you are showing a dog as it is in any endeavor. You must believe in your dog before you ever undertake the job of showing. Then you must transfer that belief so that your dog thinks it is the greatest dog that ever walked. In order to take advantage of positive psychology, you must mentally prepare every step of the way up to and into the ring.

Prior to going into the show ring during the week, sit down for ten minutes a day, close your eyes and practice putting yourself into situations that could get you into trouble. For instance, what will you do when a dog runs up on you in the ring? What will you do if the dog defecates or urinates in the ring, or rabbit hops, or the tent falls down, or the gates blow away? How will you react if you fall down in the ring, if the dog doesn't use its ears, gets too excited or not excited enough? Whatever the situation, if you have the problem solved mentally in advance, then you will know how to respond to it.

The night before a show lie in bed and think about the competition. If you've been going to shows pretty regularly, you'll have an idea of who the competition will be. You should know the strong and weak points of every dog in the ring, and if you don't know them in advance of getting to the show, stand at ringside and watch them as they come up for the class.

Think about the weather. Does your dog like the cold or shiver when a breeze blows by? If it is going to be a hot day, what will you do to keep your dog cool and comfortable?

In addition to solving all the possible problems in your head, you must visualize the picture you want to make. In order to do this, you must know your dog very well, both the strong points and the faults. Then imagine in your mind exactly how you will show the dog so that it makes a perfect picture in front of the judge. If you know your dog well, you should not have to put a hand on it in order to create the mental picture as you prepare yourself for competition.

SOLVING PROBLEMS MENTALLY

You must solve all of these potential problems mentally before you go into the ring. That takes concentration, not only the night before, but right up until the time you walk into that ring. Prior to going into the ring most professional handlers will seem to be off in space, but they're not. They're thinking about the best way to show their dog on that particular day under the unique circumstances in that ring. Most owner-handlers stand outside the ring and talk. Their dogs are out at the end of the lead, looking terrible, getting into trouble with other dogs, sitting on the wet grass or cold concrete or standing in the hot sun. Then when they take their dogs into the ring and lose, they complain about the crooked judge.

TUNNEL VISION

When you bring your dog up to the ring, you must have tunnel vision. Your total concentration is on that dog. Shut out the world and spend your time reading your dog. What is it reacting to? How does it feel that day? Is it up and happy or low and dragging? How can you compensate for those subtle changes in attitude and mood that can mean the difference between winning and losing in tough competition?

Exhibitors line up in the Westie ring and concentrate on setting their dogs up for the judge.

A judge examines a Shih Tzu on the table while the handler makes sure the dog remains in proper position.

A handler gets ready to gait her Irish Setter. Note how she thinks about controlling the dog by the specific length of lead she plans to use.

WIDE-ANGLE VISION

While you are concentrating with tunnel vision on your dog, at the same time you also have to be aware of everything that is going on around you and how it might affect your dog's performance. You must have wide-angle vision in order to evaluate the competition and to ward off any dangers that may threaten your dog. You must see that dog coming at yours and be quick enough to react. You see the person walking in a daze who may trip or fall over your dog. You can't do that if you're chatting with the neighbors or paying attention to other things.

Wide-angle vision means something else, too. It means sizing up the competition before you go into the ring or immediately after. You have to know every dog in that ring and how it compares to yours within thirty seconds. How do your dog's strengths and weaknesses compare to the others? You have to know this in order to be able to position your dog to its best advantage in the ring.

If you are given the choice of where to stand in line in the ring, you must be prepared ahead so that someone else, who is better prepared than you, will not usurp your place. You want to present the best parts of your dog so that the judge will see them from the beginning and will be able to see them every time your dog is looked at. By knowing exactly what you want to do and being positive about it *without being rude or pushy*, you will rattle the confidence of most of the other exhibitors in the ring with you.

CONCENTRATION

Many owner-handlers become intimidated by the competition. They get so nervous that they shake, and their dogs pick it up instantly. Once that happens it's all over, because you have lost that show mentally before you have ever shown your dog. If you have tunnel vision on your dog when you get into that ring, you can't be intimidated by anyone. Concentration is the key to good performance.

Years ago there was an owner-handler who got so nervous when he was in competition with the top Cocker Spaniel professional that he flubbed in every show. He just could not win because he defeated himself before ever stepping into the ring. One day, finally using tunnel vision when he got to ringside and concentrating only on the dog and the judge, he beat the professional and went Best in Show. It can be done, but it takes practice to unlearn bad habits and replace them with good ones.

A POSITIVE ATTITUDE

A positive mental attitude conveys itself instantly to the dog at the end of the lead. This is particularly true for the owner-handler who lives with a dog day and night. One time there was an elderly gentleman, about seventy-five years old, who had a Basset Hound. As he walked the Basset Hound, he was all hunched over with his head lowered. When he gaited the dog in the ring, he shuffled along and the dog would shuffle along beside him with tail down and ears dragging. Finally, he was persuaded to put a smile on his face and a little bounce in his step. Immediately the dog's tail and head came up. Previously, that man had shown that dog for a year and a half and had never won a point. Once his attitude changed, he finished the dog in six straight shows.

There's another Basset Hound story that illustrates the importance of self-confidence and attitude. In the Midwest there was a young lady who was quite a bit overweight and more than a little unsure of herself. She was a mad-at-the-world type and she showed a Basset whose tail dragged on the ground at one end and whose head was near the ground at the other. She was encouraged to try to have a better attitude toward herself and her dog. When she smiled and stepped out in a confident manner, the dog's head came up and its tail started wagging. Every time she stopped smiling, that dog's tail drooped and began to drag around the ring. The change in her attitude made a dramatic difference in the way she showed her dog and in the dog's response.

Your own psychic energy will translate itself to the dog so that your positive mental attitude will foster greater energy in the dog. The two of you as a team will fuel one another so that you both will feel better, look better and project a better image to the judge.

RESPONSE TO STRESS—A QUICK REMEDY

Mental attitude plays an essential part in your physical responses to stress and how you control your emotions. However, it is not entirely possible to hide your nervousness and apprehension from your dog.

As an owner-handler you may do all right in the classes and in Best of Breed competition, but what happens when you get into the Group, playing in the big time? How often will your dog, who has behaved perfectly all day, suddenly go to pieces before your eyes? Patches moves her feet or rabbit hops. She puts her ears back and won't stand for the judge. What happened? The dog knows you are excited by the adrenaline that is excreted in your breath. The dog smells it and thinks, ''Something is wrong with Mom or Dad,'' and she begins to react with apprehension. You can control the reaction of your dog to the additional adrenaline that your body is pumping out simply by sucking on a breath mint. That will mask the odor, and if you control your body motions, the dog will be reassured that everything is fine and will show better. A lady in Cleveland wrote to say that her dog never stood still in the ring in its life. The day she used a breath mint was the first time her dog behaved, and she won the class and went Best of Breed over seven Specials.

Speed Limit

Mental preparation is especially important when you make the cut and get down to the final competition. When your adrenaline is pumping, your actions speed up. You may think you are doing everything at normal speed, such as stacking your dog, putting on or taking off the lead, gaiting, but in reality you will have done everything at double your normal pace. This not only confuses your dog, it makes your actions jerky and will throw your dog off balance.

When you are in that situation, you must do everything half speed. When you go to set the dog's leg, do it half speed. As you gather the lead to begin your gaiting pattern, do it half speed. To you, in your excited state, it will seem like it is taking forever, but in actuality, you'll be doing things at a normal pace.

Adrenaline makes your motions less smooth and your strength increase, so that the little tug you normally give on the lead becomes a hard yank. To combat this reaction of the adrenaline, do everything half speed.

There's a dramatic example of that. A few years back a young handler had won the Group at Westminster, and he was getting ready to go into Best in Show competition. He was terrified that he would fall apart and his dog would react and fall apart, too. In that competition there is no room for error. Before it became time to go into the ring, he went back to the grooming area, sat down and thought about doing everything at half speed. He put on his jacket slowly. He walked up to the ring after everyone else was in place ready to go in for the big finish, and when the finalists were summoned into the ring, he gaited his dog perfectly. His competitors were overreacting, overdoing and generally making a mess of themselves and their dogs. He gave the finest performance of his career and his dog went Best in Show.

He did it all by doing everything half speed. He was able to do that because he took the time to think about every move in advance and to plan exactly what he was going to do and how he would do it. In the execution he had sufficient control to slow his motions down, even though his heart was pounding and adrenaline was shooting through his bloodstream.

PSYCHING THE COMPETITION

In addition to mentally preparing, or "psyching yourself," there are things you can do to psych the competition. When you are showing on the Group level, generally there are good dogs, so you have to give yourself an extra edge. Part of that edge is to unsettle the confidence of your competition.

For instance, there seems to be a great rush to be first in the ring. Why most owner-handlers want to lead the pack is a mystery. It's the hardest place in line to be, but if you want to play the game, go to the ring early and stand and wait. You will soon see people trying to edge in front of you, trying to manuever their way to the head of the line. Let them think that you're determined to be first until the class is called into the ring. Then you can suddenly turn around and say something to someone, and they will sneak by you, thinking they have put one over on you. But you will end up where you want to be and they will end up first in line.

One way to totally catch the competition off guard is to walk by someone feverishly grooming, stop, shake your head a bit and just keep walking. That will blow their minds, especially if you have just been working on your dog and you look as if you know

Grooming before you enter the ring is a great pacifier for jangled nerves. Here an exhibitor scissors her poodle.

A handler works on a Bichon Frise before show time.

what you're doing. Even if you don't know, do something by your actions to convince the competition that you know more about this business than they do.

If your competition is weak in a certain part, such as neck and shoulder, work with your dog's neck and shoulder. If it is a groomed breed, concentrate on that area while your competition is watching. They are going to get upset because you are making your dog look better and there is nothing they can do about it. You can use grooming as an outlet, both for your own anxieties and to rattle the competition. However, hide your dog from the judge as you groom.

Grooming just before you enter the show ring is a great pacifier for jangled nerves. Here you are using your tunnel vision to concentrate completely on your dog. Even if you only move one hair, you are doing something to prepare yourself mentally and to show the competition that you are doing more than they are.

EMPHASIZING FAULTS

Within thirty seconds of entering the ring you should know what is right and wrong with every dog in the ring. And you should absolutely know the best parts of your own dog. A good professional judges every dog in the class and knows exactly which dog has to be beaten.

One big mistake the owner-handler makes is to bring attention to the wrong part of the dog. As a general rule, if the dog has a bad hindquarter, for instance, the owner-handler will set the dog up, set the hindquarter and every two seconds look back to make sure that the hindquarter is set up properly. All you are doing is calling attention to that bad part of your dog. If you have a dog with a fault in a particular area, set it up once and leave it alone.

Refrain from extra movement or activity in the ring. Every move you make should enhance the presentation of the animal. If you don't have a specific reason to do something, then don't do it. Most amateurs, and quite a few professionals, fuss over their dogs, brushing, combing, whirling around their dogs, all because they are trying to overcome their nervousness. If you have prepared yourself mentally to control those nerves and to put your hands exactly where you want them, you will appear as Ms. Cool while everyone else is fidgeting around their dogs.

This exhibitor concentrates on her dog, not on the judge.

Once you set up the dog leave it alone and don't fuss.

It's the same as someone walking down the street and seeing a person looking up at the sky. Pretty soon everyone on the block is looking up at the sky. If you see someone peeking through a knothole in a fence, you work to find yourself a knothole. The human being is a curious animal, and judges being human, too, will certainly try to find out what is so interesting about that part of your dog that you are fussing with continually. Chances are good that he or she will come closer to take a look at the fault you are trying so hard to hide.

So instead of emphasizing the fault, take advantage of human curiosity and use subtle presentation to look at, stare at and admire the good part of your dog. Concentrate totally on the best features of your dog, and by inconspicuously looking at that area, you will draw the judge's eye where you want her to look.

EYE CONTACT

While you are doing this, focus on your dog, but do not make eye contact with the judge. Judges hate exhibitors who stand or kneel in front of them grinning or pleading with their eyes to choose their dog. Many classes and many wins are lost because of inappropriate eye contact with the judge. Look at your dog when the judge comes down the line to examine it.

There is only one time in which it is permissible to make eye contact with the judge. After the entire class has been examined and you are all lined up for a final time, you may look up as the judge comes to your dog, and then, once again, you should concentrate on what you want the judge to see. Inexperienced exhibitors will look at the dog and stare at the judge. You want to do the opposite. You have only one opportunity to focus your eyes on the judge, so you must time it perfectly.

Everything that you do before and during the time you are showing your dog has a mental component to it. The better you master your own thoughts, emotions and concentration, the more likely it is that your dog will show better and you will have a better chance of winning.

7

Preparation for the Ring

MOST OWNER-handlers arrive at a show and set their tack up next to friends in their breed. They groom their dogs, show, converse and leave. From this exercise they learn nothing.

Successful amateurs go early, take a chair up to ringside and watch other breeds being shown. If they are smart, they will watch the judge under whom they will be showing that day. By observing the judge's pattern, how the dogs are positioned, whether the classes are called in catalog order and, most important, what the judge seems to be looking for, observers should get ample clues as to how their breed will be judged that day.

LEARNING GROUND—THE SHOW GROUNDS

The show itself should be a learning ground. You should arrive early so that you can set yourself up in an advantageous place. If you plan to unload under the tent at an outdoor show, try to get a place near your ring. If you plan to work out of your car or van, try to park close enough to be able to see through to your ring or, in hot weather, park in the shade.

By arriving early you may be able to walk your ring, or at least observe enough to discover the potholes that can crack an ankle, note the way the sun will be moving and what the footing will be. At an indoor show, make a note of the mats or carpeting so that you will know whether you have to handle your dog in a way to compensate for slippery floors. Notice whether there are loudspeakers that can blare right into the ring and frighten your dog out of its wits.

Take a good look at the size of the ring and the pattern that the judge uses so you do not have to ask after the same thing has been explained eighty times before it is your turn to gait.

Find out from the steward how that judge will be doing Specials competition. Will it be catalog order, or, as sometimes happens in big Specials classes, catalog order with dogs in front of bitches. Some judges do not care how the dogs are brought in to the ring. Others are very particular about catalog order. They do this for two reasons. First, to make sure that no one is overlooked, and it gives the judge a sense of order. Second, it is easier for the ringside gallery to follow the action in the ring if they can identify dogs by their handlers' armbands in some semblance of order.

Do not wait until you are in the ring to find out where you should stand, because if you do that you will have lost already. If you are fumbling around looking for your place in line, you have been psyched out and the ball game is over.

ASSISTANCE AT RINGSIDE

A lot of owner-handlers make the mistake of bringing their own dogs to the ringside. Now, many have no choice if they are working alone, but there is a real advantage to having someone else hold your dog outside the ring.

You may think that professional handlers are lazy because they stand outside the ring, telling dirty jokes, watching girls in short dresses or guys in tight pants in the ring next to theirs. When the class is called, the assistant puts the lead in their hands and they walk in. It is not because they are too tired to hold the lead themselves. They do that as a psychological tool to control their dogs.

A well-trained Maltese observes the scene at an indoor show while the owner checks the ring.

This handler steadies the Pomeranian with her hands while awaiting her turn to enter the ring.

The assistant stands outside the ring, away from the handler, just keeping the dog quiet. That's all. No attention, no patting on the head or brushing or talking. Just quietly waiting. Just before it is time to enter the ring, the professional takes the dog, who is happy to see the handler. The dog knows it's show time and there will be treats and a good time in the ring.

The amount of time that you spend at ringside before your class is called will depend upon the dog itself. If you have a dog that is so exuberant that it is uncontrollable, then you will want to bring it up to ringside and stand around so that it will wear itself out just enough to behave perfectly in the ring.

Most owner-handlers do not have that problem. Usually the opposite is true, with their dogs having no go-power. That is why having someone bring the dog up to ringside for you is helpful. Your dog will see you talking to someone else and will want to be with you, so that when you take that lead and enter the ring, the dog will be up and happy.

Most owner-handlers get to ringside far too early. They may do this out of insecurity, afraid that they may miss their class, or because they want to watch the other dogs in their breed, or just to chat with the folks at ringside. This is a big mistake. Your dog will become bored and lazy and want to lie down. The dog then becomes inattentive and restless, so that by the time you go into the ring, the dog has lost all its enthusiasm and won't show. You might as well have stayed home that day, because a dog that won't show has lost before it ever gets to the ring.

If you want to watch the classes before yours, do your grooming and preparations early, go to ringside, watch a few classes, then go back and get your dog. Setting up near the ring makes that much more feasible.

THE DOG'S MENTAL ATTITUDE

While you are working with your dog before show time, notice how Star is feeling that day. Does he seem to be happy and alert, glad to be there, or a little sluggish and down? Many factors affect a dog's attitude, both in the ring and outside, and you have to know how your dog is reacting *on the day* to determine how best to show

These Irish Setters await their turn for action away from the ring at an outdoor show.

This Borzoi waits at ringside while the owners watch the proceedings. They will be able to estimate how much time they have left and familiarize themselves with the judge's gaiting pattern.

him that day. (We are obviously not talking about dogs who are sick, because they should not be on the show grounds under any circumstances.)

Read Them—and Don't Weep!

Dogs, like people, react to the weather, humidity, heat, cold, rain or sun. Bitches may act down or uncooperative during their seasons or false pregnancies.

If your dog seems especially hyper, you must try to stabilize her by a very low-key approach. Don't try to use bait, don't talk to Patches or encourage her. Use a minimum of hand motions and try to do everything smoothly and evenly.

If your dog is a little down on the day, use the opposite techniques. Play with, encourage or bait the dog, *but* do all these things in the ring. The most important thing in the making of a show dog is to teach her to be happy in the ring.

The biggest mistake an owner-handler makes when walking into the ring and starting to show is to push the dog to the limit within the first five minutes. The dog runs out of steam before even being examined by the judge. Timing is a most important part of being successful in the ring. You have to read your dog's mental attitude to know when the animal will quit so that you can save something for the end of the class.

HOT WEATHER—DOS AND DON'TS

A big part of showing a dog is adapting to the conditions on the day. There are so many variables that can affect how you and your dog act that you must practice many times under many different conditions to be able to master them all. You need to practice physically in order to get your dog accustomed to all conditions, and you need to practice mentally to overcome the problems that a given show's physical surroundings present.

The most difficult and the most dangerous condition facing the exhibitor and the dog is heat. *Preparation* for showing in the heat can make all the difference as to whether your dog will be able to show in hot weather or not. Some dogs simply cannot take the heat, so you as an owner-handler have to face that fact and stay home. *The dog's welfare comes first*, under any conditions.

Dos

There are some things you can do to make your dog more comfortable in the heat, and some things you should absolutely not do.

- Do keep your dog in a consistent temperature environment. Do not keep your dog in an air-conditioned car prior to being shown. The contrast when coming out of the cold into the heat will take all the stuffing out of your dog.

- You can use generator-run fans on the dog instead. Think of yourself in a supermarket, nice and cold, and you come walking out and the heat hits you like a brick wall. Well, dogs react 100 percent worse than people do to the change in temperature.

- At an outdoor show in the heat, arrive early and look for shade.

- If there is no shade, unload under the tent, trying to get at the end that is opposite to where the sun will be moving as it climbs higher in the middle of the day. The other important consideration in setting up at the outside edges of the tent is that you can catch any breeze that may happen by.

- Go to the ring and watch the judging procedure. If the judge is not taking exhibitors in catalog order, try to get to the front of the line. That is because you will be judged first and can stand back in the shade of the tent relaxing while others are waiting to be judged.

- If you have a judge who insists on keeping all the dogs in the sun, you have a choice. Either put your dog in the shade or ask to be excused from the class and write that show off.

- If at the end the judge asks everyone to come out into the sun for a final look, try to put yourself between your dog and the sun so that you are providing the dog with a little shade from your body.

- Spend less time grooming and fussing with your dog when it is hot.

Don'ts

There are a few common mistakes that owner-handlers make in trying to keep their dogs cool on a hot day.

- Don't wrap a dog in an ice blanket. What that does is to constrict the capillaries on the surface of the skin so that the circulatory system cannot carry heat out of the body.

- Don't allow the dog to eat ice. The transition of the cold ice into the hot dog may cause it to go into shock. You may allow your dog to lick the ice, but you are better off taking the ice cube and putting it on the throat, on the belly and around the rectum or the pads of the feet.

- Don't give the dog water just prior to going into the ring. That will make your dog logy. You are better off taking a wet towel and wiping the saliva out of the dog's mouth so that heat can be transferred from the mouth more easily.

Alcohol on the belly and applied to the pads of the feet help to cool a hot dog because of the rapid evaporation. However, nothing will evaporate when the humidity is very high, and the danger of heat stroke intensifies as humidity rises.

If you are in the ring and you feel that your dog is starting to lose balance, open the mouth. If the gums are bright red, and the eyes are red around the pupils, get out of the class. Do not throw the dog into a bucket with ice. Use *cool* water and *immediately* remove the dog to a shady spot. Call the veterinarian and if possible put your dog into an air-conditioned car and go straight to a vet if there is one nearby.

If a dog decides to quit in the heat, let the dog quit. Don't force any animal for the sake of a ribbon, because even if you don't kill the dog, you certainly will have ruined any chance of it showing for you in the heat again.

A motor home provides shade and protection under the awning and self-contained comfort from the elements.

Mats at indoor shows can sometimes be slippery. This is a class where handlers are learning to stack their dogs to prepare for that condition.

If you are walking to the ring and the dog starts to throw up, turn around and go home.

Black dogs are more vulnerable than any others, except for the short-nosed breeds, like Bulldogs and Pugs. How many times have you seen people with their black Labs, when the temperature is 100 degrees, standing in the sun with their dogs. Then they expect them to go into the ring and show.

Do not use any of the products on the coat with ingredients that make the coat shine. If you put anything on the dog, like alcohol, it will burn the coat. These products suck in the heat even more because they act like a magnifying glass on the coat.

Sometimes if a dog is not suffering, but just seems a little logy in the ring, you can psych it into showing for you despite the heat. There was a Springer who really did not like the heat. His tail would be down and he would plod along. The handler decided to trick the dog, so he had his children bundle up in jackets and stand at his crates, pretending to shiver, and throw little pieces of white paper into the air, saying "Look, it's snowing." The dog picked himself up and showed himself to a Best in Show. He may not have been the smartest dog in the world, but the psychology helped him win and he didn't feel the heat.

FOOTING

The type of footing you are on can make the difference between win and lose, so you have to prepare ahead to compensate for slippery floors. You can learn from others by watching at ringside or asking questions of professionals who have faced those problems before you.

There's a good example that came out of a show in New York. It was the Combined Setter Specialty when it was held at the old Statler Hilton. The floors were carpeted but slick. Everyone's dogs were sliding; no one could get a firm stack no matter what they put on their dogs' feet or how they positioned them. During Junior Showmanship competition, a little girl, faced with the same problem, took her show lead, folded it twice and laid it on the carpet. She placed her dog's back feet on the lead and they stayed firm.

Later in the day, during Specials competition, one handler who happened to watch juniors that day, took her example and used the lead to position the dog's hind feet. His was the only dog that didn't slide and he went Best of Breed that day.

Many years later that little trick, done by an unsuspecting but savvy junior, helped a handler win the Group at Westminster and later to go on to Best in Show.

Study your conditions in advance and try to work out solutions for the problems ahead of time.

As these multiple Best-in-Show bitches from Alekai prove, regardless of what is in fashion, the impeccably groomed entry has an advantage in any ring.

8

Grooming for
the Show Ring

GROOMING is a very, very important aspect of preparation for the show ring. It does not matter if you have a long-coated breed such as an Old English Sheepdog, one which takes four hours to brush out properly for the ring, or a Doberman Pinscher, which is referred to as a wash-and-wear, drip-dry dog. Grooming is an ongoing process, from the time your dog is a puppy. You will have plenty of time to experiment with different shampoos, conditioners and tools, but the most important element in a healthy coat is a healthy dog.

There are grooming implements for every type of coat imaginable, from the short-haired Dalmatian to the Old English Sheepdog. You will have to select the tools which are correct for your breed. Take the advice of the breeder from whom you purchased your dog. Or, go to shows and watch as your breed is being groomed. Ask a knowledgeable person to show you how to care for and groom your dog.

All basic grooming is done at home. You don't want to upset a dog who is jittery about its feet by cutting nails just before you take the dog into the ring. Grooming should be a pleasant experience at a show. Ears should have been cleaned at home and the dog freshly bathed the day before a show. Many exhibitors bathe their dogs at home and wrap them in bath towels until it is time for them to be done out at the show. Some wrap to keep the hair flat in addition to keeping the coat spotless and free of dust and dirt.

Anything that you do to **naturally** enhance the appearance of your dog is acceptable. The condition of the coat and the finesse of the trimming, where it is permitted, often play a part when there is a close decision between two dogs of equal worth. You want your dog to look its best, because this is a reflection of the care and attention that you have given.

There are, unfortunately, people who will do anything to win. They have forgotten (if they ever knew) that the purpose of a dog show is to show off one's best breeding stock, to compare their dogs with others of the same breed and to receive the opinion of a judge on any particular day. Layered onto this basic and original purpose is the fact that we are attending a dog "show." So that, just as we would go to any occasion dressed in our best clothes, we try to present our dogs in their best light.

Unfortunately, to some people this means falsifying those things they would have liked Nature to have changed for them. Dogs are presented dyed different colors. Terriers have dark saddles painted on where they didn't exist. Yorkies miraculously become steel grey and ruddy tan. Irish Setters become solid red from nose to tail. Other cosmetic enhancements are done also, from changing the way a tail is carried to fixing bad bites, adding a missing testicle or correcting faulty ear sets.

All of these things are illegal, and if challenged by a fellow exhibitor or a judge and found to be true, the dog may be permanently disqualified by AKC from ever being shown again, all awards will be rescinded and the owner will be severely penalized. Unfortunately, many of these practices go undetected or unproven, so the dog finishes its championship and is bred to the bitch of some unsuspecting breeder. The cleverly hidden faults appear in the next generation, to the dismay of the poor breeder who has been taken in. For the sake of winning, deceitful exhibitors are willing to jeopardize the future of their breeds.

Although these practices are not widespread, they do appear often enough for concerned breeders and exhibitors to be aware of them. Owner-handlers and professionals are equally guilty of malpractice, so there is plenty of blame to spread around. Only if judges and exhibitors protest and speak out will these unethical procedures be stopped.

Not only does the process of grooming regularly enhance the beauty of the dog, but, if done properly, it will enhance the mental attitude of the dog. If you spend time washing, brushing, trimming, rubbing, smoothing, polishing, combing and whatever else is done to make the dog look the best that it can, the attitude in this process is easily transferred. It will give your dog a completely different feeling than if you just yank the dog out of the car and run into the show ring.

It's the same thing as going into a beauty salon and having a complete makeover. You walk out feeling like a million dollars, and yet, in actuality, you are exactly the same person. But the way you feel about yourself is totally different.

If you don't think this is true, there are two little activities you can engage in to prove this. Park outside a beauty salon and watch the people go in, and then watch them come out. Be aware of their attitudes going into the shop and the difference in their carriage and behavior as they walk away.

Carry this to the canine world. Go to your local grooming parlor and watch the dogs as they are brought in and later picked up by their owners. Observe the attitude, not only of the dogs, but also of the owners as they take their dogs. You can see the pride and pleasure that the owner takes in a freshly bathed and groomed pet, and the animals, too, are perkier and proud of themselves as they prance out.

Coated breeds are brushed out thoroughly. Straggly hairs are removed and final touch-up scissoring may be done. Some breeds have their furnishings bathed at the show and are blow dried. When using a blow dryer, it is advisable to use only forced air or warm air, never hot, as this will dry out the coat.

Touch-up work at a show for short-haired dogs consists of trimming whiskers, cleaning and polishing the coat, washing and drying the legs and feet and using whatever natural whitener is permitted on dogs with white socks and markings.

Spending time grooming at a show will help enhance the feeling that you have done everything possible to make your dog the very best it can be. If you feel confident about this, it will go right down the lead to the dog.

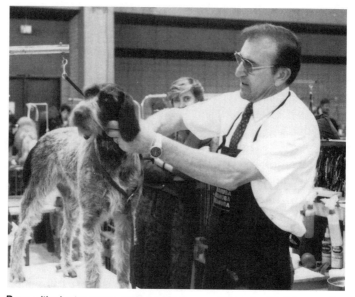

Dogs with shorter coats, such as this German Wirehaired Pointer, need considerable preparation time also.

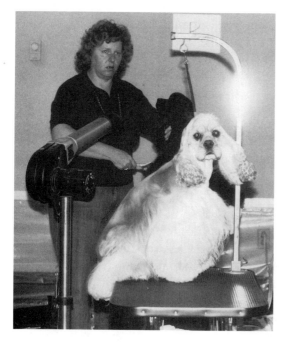

This Cocker Spaniel is being blow-dried. For breeds with profuse coat, a hair dryer is part of tack box equipment.

There is a good example of this. A youth went to work for a famous Boxer handler, a natural thing since he was raised with Boxers. He assumed there was very little grooming or preparation on a Boxer for the show ring because of the short hair. Basic grooming, such as bathing, ear cleaning and nail trimming were done at the kennel. He was amazed at the physical preparation on that dog at the shows, and he could see a noticeable change in the mental attitude of the dog during this process. The lessons he learned from that experience were among the most important influences on that young handler during his career.

INSIDE—OUTSIDE

You will be showing under different conditions indoors and outdoors. If you have a long-coated breed, this will make a difference in your grooming preparations for the ring.

As a general rule, you will show a dog with less feathering at outdoor shows than at indoor ones. As an example, a handler at one of the Irish Setter National Specialties walked his dog up to ringside just prior to entering the Specials ring. His dog was in magnificent coat with feathering almost to the ground. He looked at the ring and saw that the grass was between four and five inches high. He sent his assistant back to the crates to get a pair of thinning shears, and there at ringside proceeded to cut three to four inches off the belly coat of the dog. Yes, he won the National Specialty and the judge's comment was that his was one of the few dogs that showed any leg under it. All the other Irish Setters looked very short-legged and close to the ground. The judge said obviously the breed is in trouble. Actually, it was not so obvious, since most of the other dogs would not have appeared so short-legged with some judicious grooming.

You have to adapt to your ring conditions. However, if you are showing at one outdoor show and twenty indoor shows, you would not trim for the one show. Use common sense.

There are times when your grooming and presentation must be focused for a particular judge. A good example of this occurred with two Gordon Setters which were shown many years ago.

Yankee was a very elegant, streamlined, Irish Setter type of Gordon. He carried a tremendous amount of hair and had long ears.

He was a rangy dog. Tory, on the other hand, was a compact, Gordon-type of dog. He did not have a lot of hair and was shorter in body and in body type. Both had won Groups and Bests in Show, and both would go in and out of coat at no specific times of the year. Yankee was shown on a drop loose lead and Tory was shown on an up lead behind the ears.

One year just before the Gordon Setter Specialty in New York, Tory lost all his top coat. The judge was one who loved the dog and who had given him many wins. So I took Yankee and trimmed him to look like Tory. I cut off his ear feathers and trimmed up his belly coat and furnishings and showed him with the lead up under his ears. I won the Specialty and as the judge handed me the ribbon, he said, "Tory never looked better."

The following year we had a judge who loved Yankee, but Yankee had been out hunting all season. He had lost weight and hair and was just not in show condition. I trimmed Tory to look like Yankee and showed him on a drop loose lead like an Irish Setter. As the judge handed me the BOB ribbon he said, "Yankee never looked better."

There are many times when you have to trim your dog for what you know the judge will like. English judges of Sporting dogs are accustomed to seeing more top coat and less severe trimming than American judges. At one show an English judge was doing Irish Setters and I had let my client's dog grow two weeks worth of hair, so that she looked somewhat ungroomed. She won Winners Bitch and Best of Opposite Sex, but the client was indignant that I had shown what she considered to be an untrimmed dog. The next week she was shown with a haircut in the usual way.

Judges, especially those of long experience, are very precise in how they want a dog presented to them. Judges such as Percy Roberts and Alva Rosenberg, and today's senior judges like Tom Gately, Henry Stoecker and William Kendrick know exactly how they want a dog trimmed and presented in its particular breed. They are very definite on how the head and tail should be placed, how the neck should fit into the shoulders and how the dog should be trimmed for its breed.

It also happens that judges change their opinions of how a dog should be presented. At one point styles that they might have considered excellent trim, condition and presentation, might now be considered overtrimmed, overpresented, and even overconditioned. Handlers must learn to adjust to the judges' changing patterns over time.

There was a judge of Sporting dogs who truly hated short toenails. If a dog came into her ring with very short nails, which most show dogs have, it would go to the end of the line immediately. Exhibitors who knew this fetish let their dogs' nails grow for about a month before showing to this person. Immediately afterward all the nails went back to their normal length.

GETTING ADVICE

While you are perfecting the grooming techniques applicable to your particular breed, it is wise to set up next to a successful owner or professional handler at a show in order to watch how they go about grooming their dogs. If any of the information you pick up is useful, then try it on your own dog. *Be very cautious*, however, *about copying specific grooming techniques* for your dog unless you know why that handler is using them. *What is good for one dog may not be right for another*.

Do not ever be afraid to ask a handler why a particular grooming technique is used on a certain dog. Handlers usually will not be happy about entertaining general questions, such as, ''How can I groom (or show) my dog better?'' If you ask a vague or nonspecific question, the handler will assume that you are not really ready to learn, and you will get only vague answers.

THINK GOOD THOUGHTS

During the grooming process, however long it takes, use the time to mentally prepare your dog for the ring. Assess your dog's mental attitude and your own feelings on the day. If your dog is up too high during the grooming session, use the time to relax the dog and bring dog and handler under control. If you both are down and not alert, gradually try to increase your own enthusiasm level, so that by the time the dog is ready to come off the table and go into the ring, you are both up and showing.

FINAL THOUGHTS

Do not do any basic maintenance at a show. All nail trimming, whisker trimming and mat pulling should be done at home. Any grooming that the dog finds unpleasant should have been done in advance so that the preparation at the show is a pleasurable experience for the dog. You cannot take a dirty, matted, ungroomed animal to a show and expect to turn it into a perfect specimen on the spot.

The minimum amount of time spent preparing a dog for the show ring at a show is a half hour. This is absolute, and even applies to short-haired dogs, such as Min Pins and Doberman Pinschers. As the hair grows longer, so does the preparation time. It is appalling to see some exhibitors, amateur and professional, take a dog out of the crate and walk it to the ring to compete against a real professional who has just spent an hour or more preparing the dog for competition.

Preparation for the show ring is both physical and mental. Every step should be planned and executed according to a timetable that you carry in your mind. If you do this, you will develop the finesse necessary to be a successful competitor.

9

When You Are
in the Ring

$\mathbf{B}$ASIC TRAINING of your puppy begins at home. You teach the pup to walk on a show lead, to trot, to stack for short periods of time. But the main training of your show dog is done in the ring. You want to find out how your dog responds to different stimuli, and you can only do that by trial and error in the ring. You want your dog to be happy in the ring, and the only way to find out what makes the dog happy is go out there and try it.

In addition to the physical setting of the show itself, there are so many variables that influence the way your dog will react that you must allow yourself the time and the experiences to investigate what makes your dog look best.

ANALYZING A DOG'S GAIT

How many people actually analyze their dog's gait before they begin to show it? Most people decide on a show lead without giving any thought to how it will make the dog look while it is moving. They use a choke or a slip collar or a martingale without really

The most common lead position is where the lead is held upright, directly behind the ears with pressure from above.

With the lead behind the ears the pressure comes from a forward position in this drawing.

Lead pressure can also come from the rear.

looking at their dog. To find out how your dog looks, have someone else gait it for you, up and down and around, just as you would in the show ring.

You will find, after observing and experimenting with different leads and different ways of holding each lead, that your dog will look better some ways than others. Yet most people are so set in their ways that they never think that the difference between winning and losing may be as simple as a change of lead.

The secret of showing a dog successfully is in the control of the head. Just as the secret of showing a horse is control of the head through the bit in its mouth, a dog is controlled by a lead around its neck.

LEAD POSITIONS

There are about twenty different ways that you can position the lead that will make a difference in the way your dog gaits.

The most common lead position is where the lead is held upright, directly behind the dog's ears with pressure from above. Some dogs gait very well that way, but others will fight the lead if they feel that pressure. In the upright position, you can hold the head directly above the dog's neck, or you can hold it forward or in back of the dog's head. Each position will change the gait for better or for worse.

You can position the lead halfway down the neck, and some dogs will respond to that by driving into the lead, extending their reach in front by several inches.

Another way to place the lead is to the side, and here, again, it can be tight or loose, slightly forward and straight out or behind the dog's head.

While you are gaiting your dog, in every breed except the Miniature Pinscher, you want the legs to form an ''A'' when you are observing lateral movement. The dog's forequarters and hindquarters should be in balance, like two triangles, front and rear. When you see a dog trotting free, you will see that, if the dog is made correctly, the front legs and rear legs will have an equal amount of reach and follow-through in the front and in the rear. When you put a lead around the dog's neck, that changes the center of gravity, so you must find the type of lead, the position and the

You can position the lead halfway down the neck.

The lead can sometimes be placed at the bottom of the neck.

Here the lead comes up on the side of the head, behind the ears.

amount of pressure that will allow the dog to maintain that free and balanced stride. Some dogs, depending upon the breed, will have greater or lesser reach and drive, but if they are made correctly they will be equal in the length of their front and rear stride.

HANDLER'S STRIDE

There's another element besides the type and position of the lead that will influence your dog's gait: the length of the handler's stride. You can run with little mincing steps or walk with a short, choppy stride, and no matter how good the dog's gait appears when running in the backyard, your dog will look terrible in the show ring. You have to practice lengthening your stride so that your dog moves along smoothly with you.

Just as the way you move your legs and body affect the lead and the dog's reaction to it, you also have the choice of going slow, medium speed or fast. Each of those will influence your dog's gait.

You may find that your dog gaits better with the lead held in a certain way that the handler (or you) has not normally used. Do you then adjust yourself to what the dog wants, or do you teach the dog to accept the lead and gait evenly in a different way? Obviously the answer should be: Teach the dog to do it the way the gait looks best. That takes time and many shows before the two of you will become a team that works together under all conditions.

PLACE IN LINE

Where you are placed in line is very important. Being first may be an advantage or a disadvantage, depending upon your dog and the circumstances of the day.

We mentioned the advantage of the lead position in line on a very hot day, but in general, first is the worst place to be, especially for someone who has trouble setting up a dog quickly. To be first your dog practically has to set up by itself instantly. Otherwise you will be fumbling around as the judge approaches to look at your dog.

Aside from the mechanics of stacking your dog in line, there are other important considerations. Most of them fall into the cate-

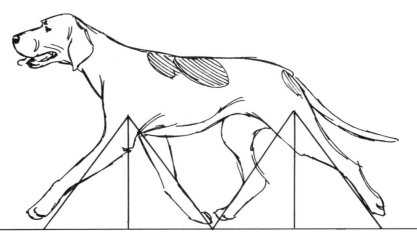

When viewed from the side, the dog's forequarters and hindquarters should be in balance, each pair like a triangle, front and rear.

This handler and English Springer Spaniel are perfectly synchronized.

gory of common sense. Unless the judge wants the class in catalog order, put your dog where it looks the best.

If you have a dog with a head that looks as if it was hit with an ugly stick, with big yellow eyes that could be used for airport landing lights, where would you put that dog? In the front of the line, because the judge spends most of the evaluation time in the middle of the ring, and from that position the judge can't see your dog's terrible head.

What if your dog has poor hindquarters? You'd go to the end of the line, because in order to see that part of your dog, the judge is going to have to go way out of the way.

If your dog has a great topline, stand in the middle of the line, where the judge can't help but notice it while moving down the line.

Of course, your dog will be individually examined and obvious faults are often difficult to hide, but there's no sense in letting the judge see more of your dog's faults than is absolutely necessary.

CONTROLLING THE EXCITEMENT LEVELS

What is the first thing that happens when you walk into a ring? You stack your dog. Yet most owner-handlers stand outside the ring, baiting their dogs, getting them wired up and all excited about going into the ring. Then ten seconds later the dog is asked to stand like a statue. It's like starting your car off from a traffic light. You start slowly and keep increasing your speed. Owner-handlers go into the ring at full speed and the dog runs out of gas at the end.

You have to start slowly and build. When you get into very large classes, you don't want to push your dog until the very end. If you have a breed where the ears are supposed to be up, don't wear your dog out so the ears are coming out of the side of the head. Boxers, for instance, are supposed to have their ears up, so you see the owner-handler come in, waving the liver around, up and down, so that by the end of the class the dog is yawning. Build your dog's excitement level slowly, and if you don't make the cut in a big class, don't push the dog. You're not going to make the cut every time, so why wear the dog out? If you don't make the cut, stand there and play with your dog. Make it fun, so the next time you ask the dog to do something, you'll both feel good about it.

When you're in Group competition, you have to start all over again. Begin slowly and build as the circumstances warrant. Very rarely does one see a professional handler's dog run out of gas. A handler knows most judges' procedures and always saves something for the end. The judge makes the decisions at the end, often on the last go-around, and that's when your dog has to look its best.

TRANSITION

Transition is the hardest thing for a dog to understand. The transition from stacking to gaiting that we discussed earlier in this book is the same as the transition from high level energy to low.

The more you keep bringing your dog all the way up and all the way down like a seesaw, the faster the dog is going to get tired of it and hate it. By the end of the class your dog can't figure out what the devil you want, so the dog is going to quit. You do this enough times in the ring and you will have a deadhead.

The dogs that are campaigned over a long period of time are able to keep the pace because their handlers make those transitions from high to low as small as possible.

Ring procedures are always the same. You get your dog excited before entering the ring. You bring the dog in and go into a stack, so you are putting on the brakes. Then you gait in a circle, so you want your dog up and animated. You've changed directions twice within two minutes. The dog can't understand this. You can change this by bringing the dog in low and calm, stacking and then gaiting around the ring as you gradually build the pace and excitement.

Unless you are first in line, you will have time to calm your dog for the next stack, which will be the individual examination. At this point the dog must be the most stable in the stack during the examination. From then on you can gradually increase the excitement level, because the judge will be looking for animation and personality on the individual gaiting pattern.

However, you cannot allow the dog to get too wired, because considerable stability is required in order to gait properly in whatever pattern the judge has chosen. By the end of the class, if you know your dog well and have pushed all the right buttons to get Star up and showing, he will be charging out and looking like a million dollars, just as the judge makes a decision and points.

Remember that your whole purpose is to create a consistent

This diagram illustrates the incorrect way of building the excitement level. You do not want to gear a dog up or down drastically or you will create confusion.

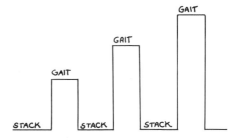

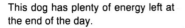

This illustration shows the correct way to building a dog's excitement level, so that it has energy left for the final moments.

This dog has plenty of energy left at the end of the day.

picture so that the dog looks the same all the time, even though you are manipulating moods and excitement levels from low and calm to high and just under control.

The whole scenario changes if you have a class of three, as compared to a large class or in the Group. In a small class you must have your dog on a fairly high level all the time, though stable enough to be examined and gaited without losing control.

Adjusting Energy—Pressing the Right Buttons

Adjusting the dog's energy level to be calm and controlled at the beginning of the class and up and animated at the end requires knowing your dog's moods and what is inside your dog's head on a particular day. We have to return to thinking about the dog's buttons. What does the dog like and what stimuli will bring the correct response consistently?

Some dogs will jump straight up in the air if you scratch their bellies. Others will say, "Oh, I like that," as they collapse in a relaxed heap.

There was a famous English Springer Spaniel who wouldn't get his tail up. Four handlers couldn't finish him, but the fifth found his button. He discovered that if he pulled on the dog's chest feathers, it made the dog furious. His tail came up and he charged around the ring. Using that simple button, the dog became the top Springer in the country.

Another Springer responded to the handler's working with the dog's tail. The handler used the tail like a gear shift. If he wanted the dog to go along slow and steady, he just picked him up by the tail a few inches off the ground and dropped him. If he wanted the dog to go faster, he twisted the tail. The more he twisted the tail, the faster the dog went. On the other hand, another dog of the same breed reacted just the opposite. The minute the handler grabbed his tail, the dog froze.

Bait is a good external stimulus, but it has to be used correctly. If you know that your dog reacts in a frenzy to a certain type of bait, say pork liver, don't show the liver just prior to going into the ring when you want your dog steady and under control. However, if the dog isn't acting happy or animated, show the liver to build up motivation before you go into the ring.

Owner-handlers often have to reprogram their dogs to enjoy

the show ring because they have made a botch of it the first time. Professional handlers make a living from owners who have destroyed their dog's enjoyment of the show ring, so they turn them over to someone else to undo the damage. There is no need for this if you will use common sense and patience in teaching your dog to love the ring.

A perfect example of this was a dog who became the top Sporting dog in the country for two years running. He was perfect running in the backyard or standing outside the ring waiting to go in. His tail would be wagging and he'd be up and perky. The minute he walked through those gates, the tail went down and that dog refused to show. His owners had been so hard on him in the ring that he learned to hate it. It took six months for the professional to undo the damage and to make that dog love the show ring.

How did he do it? By finding the buttons that made the dog tick, and by making it *fun* for that dog in the ring. The dog was fed, praised and petted in the ring and ignored outside the ring. He finally realized that it was fun to be a show dog, but how much better for dog and handlers if he had been taught properly from the beginning.

NEW EXPERIENCES

Every experience is new for a dog, from puppyhood on, and you must prepare your dog for every eventuality in the ring. For instance, many shows have loudspeaker systems that blare just above the rings. For dogs unaccustomed to the sound, that is a frightening experience. Take your dog to the ringside long before your class is called. Walk around the grounds. Make sure to stand close to the loudspeakers as they blast out the national anthem, so that when you are showing in the ring the dog is already used to the noise and has learned that it is not a threat.

The same principle applies to flapping tents. Outdoor shows in many parts of the country have tents for shade. When it is windy and the tent poles start shaking and the flaps crack in the breeze, many dogs freak out. The only way to condition your dogs to ignore the tents is to take them to shows and walk them under the tents, especially when it is windy. If they begin to act anxious and cowering, do not reassure them that it is all right. By doing that you are reinforcing their behavior. You want to walk around calmly,

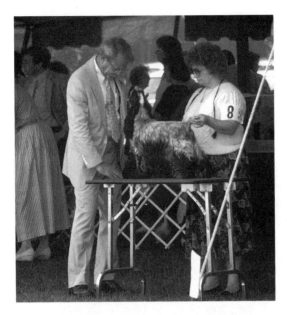

English Cocker Spaniel being examined under the tent close to spectators, a new experience which may make a young dog nervous.

Judge examines a Bullmastiff on the individual stack. Note how the handler does not fuss with the dog, but allows the judge freedom to give the dog a complete examination while maintaining a natural posture for both dog and handler.

push whatever button has made them feel good in the past and act as normally as possible. Your attitude will reassure your dogs more than making a fuss over them. This does not work for every dog. Puppies especially need some reassurance that everything is OK, but be careful *not* to reward them for acting in a frightened manner.

OBSERVATION AND STUDY—DOING YOUR HOMEWORK

Observation is key to winning. You have to go to a lot of shows and watch a lot of judges to see what type of dogs they are putting up.

Owner-handlers are the biggest gripers in the world. They complain about not winning and yet they go to a show with an untrained dog and present it to a judge who has never put up their type of dog.

If you have a tall, rangy Labrador with a hard topline that is not forty pounds overweight, would you take it to a judge who consistently puts up short-legged, fat, sway-backed dogs? Yet owners do it all the time and then complain about losing. You must do your homework before you spend your entry fees to show to a judge who is not going to like your type of dog.

At a show in Ohio there was an English judge who liked English Springer Spaniels with heads that looked like two halves of a peach with a groove down the middle. The handler, at the back of the line, kept spitting on his thumb and running it down the skull, making a groove. Someone in front of him asked what he was doing. "Winning this class," the handler said. The other man thought he was kidding until he won Best of Breed over twelve Specials. The judge said, "This is the only dog with the proper head with the groove down the middle."

The next day the handler did the same thing with his dog, and saw that everyone else in the class was copying what he was doing. Just before his turn to go out, he took his comb, knocked out the groove and showed his dog to Winners Dog. As he took the ribbon, the judge said, "You know, those were the ugliest dogs I've ever seen. Every single one had a groove down the middle of their heads."

The moral of the story: Know your judges and don't copy what someone else is doing in the ring unless it is right for your dog.

RING CONDITIONS

We have touched on the importance of knowing how to react quickly to ring conditions, some of which may change during the course of the day. For instance, if you are judged early in the morning, there will be dew on the grass, which may make it slick. Your dog may be a hothouse flower and not like the feel of the wet grass on its feet. You will have to adjust your gait *and* the dog's gait to accommodate that.

If you win Best of Breed, you will have to wait around for the Group, which is judged later in the day. You will find a different set of conditions. The ground will be dry, and sometimes dusty, or if it has been raining during the day, there will be puddles and mud to contend with.

If it is an indoor show, the mat conditions will vary from early morning to afternoon. In the morning they may be clean and hold the footing of the dogs better. By afternoon, with many dogs dropping hair on the mats and people throwing liver around the rings, the footing and the scents on mats will be different.

Ringside will be different, too. Early morning classes have relatively few spectators, but by afternoon the gallery is sometimes five or six deep, with people picnicking, talking, smoking and clapping, kids running around and other dogs standing outside the ring. Your dog has to become accustomed to all those distractions and learn to ignore them. That takes practice which can only be done in the show ring.

MEETING CHALLENGES IN THE RING

You have to mentally prepare for all sorts of other eventualities, too.

Suppose someone runs up on you in the ring, what do you do? Turn around and nicely ask the person not to disturb your dog. If it happens again, repeat your request, but in a loud voice so that the judge can hear you. That usually is enough to make a rude exhibitor back off.

If someone sets their dog up too close to you from behind, and is interfering with your dog, apologize for not leaving enough room behind you for the other exhibitor to set up the dog. This sarcasm might get their attention! If this appears to be happening a second time, stop, leaving three extra feet between you and the person in front of you. Just as the person crowding you from behind starts to work to set his or her dog, move up into the space you have left for yourself.

If your dog gallops or rabbit hops in the ring, stop and get your dog's attention. Then continue at a more controlled speed. It is perfectly acceptable to go about a quarter of the way into the gaiting pattern, stop and return. Do not do the whole pattern and then expect the judge to allow you to repeat it entirely.

Do not be embarrassed about stopping in order to get control of your dog. You should be worried only about the presentation of your dog, not about what other people are saying about you.

If you are in the ring with your dog and you notice that a judge appears to be particularly hard-handed on the dogs, it is not incorrect, as the judge approaches your dog, to ask in a polite manner for the judge to be gentle with your dog. You may explain that the dog is young and inexperienced. Most judges will respect this. If they do not, write them off and do not go back to show under that person again.

If your dog gets too excited in the ring, mentally conjure up those buttons you have been finding during the training process. If the dog does not respond to one thing, try something else. Maybe your dog will respond to that cute Poodle sitting ringside.

In order to understand how to show a dog to its best advantage to a particular judge, you must watch that judge over a period of time. Then you must practice showing your dog in the way that you see is pleasing to that judge. Not only must you train and trim the dog so that it looks good to you, but sometimes you must change the presentation for a specific judge. You may know that a dog looks better on a drop loose lead, but if a judge prefers a tight lead, you have to change your way of showing and you must practice with your dog so that it looks natural.

One way to learn how to do this is to watch a top specimen in your breed being shown by an excellent handler. You may see the dog being shown the same way nine times, but on the tenth time the dog is shown totally differently. It should become clear to you what the handler is trying to achieve. How is the handler trying to change the dog's appearance in order to comply with how the judge wishes that dog to be presented?

The handler, whether amateur or professional, must use many mental tools to change a dog's appearance for a particular judge.

MENTAL TOOLS

You have a toolbox of particular stimuli that you have learned about your dog. This is the time that you use that toolbox. When you are working on a car and you find that a small screwdriver doesn't work correctly, maybe a big screwdriver will. Don't be afraid to use another tool.

When you are doing your mental practice, reflect over all the different tools that you have. Consider the different responses that your dog gives you under certain circumstances, whether it be high stress or low stress situations. Try to mentally anticipate how you feel your dog will react to doing certain things.

If you thought about all these tools beforehand, they will be at the edge of your mind and you will be able to use them in the ring. This is like a telephone lineman crawling up on a pole. He has a tool belt with all the needed tools right there. When he needs a specific tool to do a job, he has it at hand and doesn't have to climb all the way down the pole to get the tool out of his truck.

So it is with mental preparedness for the ring. If you have solved all the potential problems in your mind, you will have the confidence to show your dog to the best of your ability.

What mental tools do you have in your box to bring out at the proper moment?

Through the months of working with your dog you know how it will react to different stimuli. You know, for instance, whether bait is a consistent tool, or one to use only when the dog is relaxed and alert.

You know how it will react to the lead and you can use the various lead positions you have learned to make the dog move in a certain way. You will sometimes see a professional handler position

118

the lead up behind the ears when gaiting the dog on the individual pattern, but drop the lead down the neck and to the side for the go-around. Changing lead positions in this way gives the dog a signal to lengthen its stride and pick up speed for the longer pattern. Many owner handlers copy the professionals in changing lead positions without knowing why they are doing this, and without practicing beforehand. They throw the dogs off balance, causing them to tilt their heads and crab around the ring.

Don't try something new in the ring and surprise your dog. You must know ahead of time whether a particular tool will be the right one for the job and whether it will give you an advantage over the competition in the ring.

Every mental tool must be used with a specific purpose in mind. Your tools are the lead you use and the way you use it, the bait you carry, the buttons you have learned work best on your dog in different situations, and your own mental attitude and confidence are important before you enter the ring and while you are in competition. Every day is different, every dog is different and there are endless combinations of dogs and handlers using mental prowess to get the winning edge over you, the competition.

Win or lose, good sportsmanship makes a show more enjoyable for everyone.

J. S. Dorl, American Kennel Club

10

Etiquette and Sportsmanship

DOG SHOWING is a sport. True, professional handlers make a living showing dogs, but the majority of exhibitors show their dogs for fun, not profit. Good professional handlers, like good baseball, football or basketball players, follow the rules of sportsmanship. To play the game fairly and honestly one has to abide by those rules.

In dog showing there are two codes of sportsmanship. One applies to your fellow exhibitors. The other applies to the judge.

SPORTSMANSHIP IN THE RING

Sportsmanship in the show ring involves more than the obvious. One does not position one's dog to deliberately block the dog in front of or behind you in line. One does not run up on the dog in front, nor stop short in order to throw the dog behind off balance. One does not attempt to distract other dogs with squeaky toys or obvious displays of bait being thrown around the ring. If your dog baits best on a squeaky toy, use it unless a competitor complains that it is distracting his dog. If that happens, use the toy, but do not make noises with it.

Exhibitors who brag about their dog before or after it is shown are in extremely bad taste. Don't tell the world that a certain judge loves your dog and that you can't lose under her. Not only are you setting yourself up for disappointment, but your comments reflect badly on the judge.

Do not stand at ringside running off at the mouth about the awful dogs in the ring. The person next to you probably owns one of them. Keep your comments to yourself, even if you are sure you should have won that class. Wait until you get into your car, roll up the windows and then vent your gripes.

If your dog loses, do not take it out on the dog. It is not the dog's fault. If it does not behave in the ring, you have not trained it. If it does not show well, you have not taught it. If it is a poor specimen and deserved to lose, you should have known that and left it home. There is absolutely no excuse for ever physically or mentally abusing a dog for any reason, least of all because it did not win a ribbon.

If you win, whether it be a Puppy class or Best of Winners, accept your ribbon politely, thank the judge and leave the ring. If you lose, leave the ring without comment. If you get a fourth out of four, accept the ribbon and thank the judge. Do not berate the judge, stomp on the ribbon or throw it into the garbage can. Not only are you demonstrating extremely poor sportsmanship, but you may be called up on charges and suspended by the American Kennel Club.

ETIQUETTE TOWARD THE JUDGE

If you are really interested in the opinion of the judge under whom you have lost, and you would like to find out why, you may engage the judge in conversation. Wait until their assignment is completed and then approach them. You can explain that you would like to discuss East Asian Hairless Hounds with them. Then at a convenient time during the day, sit down and talk about the breed without mentioning your dog. Most judges will not discuss an exhibit, except in the most general terms. If you ask why the judge didn't put your dog up, the answer will most likely be, "Because I liked the other dog better." You will have learned nothing and annoyed the judge. But if you want that person's opinion about the breed in general, you will learn where their emphasis lies by listening to what they have to say about the breed.

A judge may know there is a problem in a certain breed and therefore will pick dogs that are felt will compensate for that problem. For instance, in Toys, if there is a problem with oversize, a judge may put up dogs that are close to the lower end of the height scale for that breed. You have to know where that judge is coming from. Suppose a judge saw a whole lot of Shih Tzus that were so big they looked like Lhasas, and the Parent Club for the breed has issued a statement warning about oversized Shih Tzus. The next time that person judges the breed, the smaller dogs will be picked in order to make a statement about that breed.

In order to understand what a judge may have liked or disliked about your dog, you must be able to honestly evaluate your dog compared to others in the ring. Perhaps every dog that placed in the class was tall and rangy and your dog is short and cobby. If you were observant, you would know right away that your chances aren't good that day. In fact, unless you are in the first Puppy class, you should know by the time you walk into the ring whether the judge likes your type of dog.

POLITICS

Many owner-handlers complain about politics in the show ring. The most often heard gripe is that the handlers always win. Well, *there are politics in everything in life*, and that is a fact that the owner-handler has to recognize. However, the amateur often has an advantage over the professional because a judge is going to be more forgiving if an amateur makes a mistake, sets a dog up imperfectly or gaits awkwardly. If the dog is worthy, the judge will usually give that owner-handler every opportunity. Not so for the professional. The judges often look for the professionals to make a mistake, and they will not forgive as easily when a mistake is made here.

It is possible to promote your dog by chatting with the judges, but a better way to achieve the judge's recognition is to let the judges talk to you about the dog.

There's no question that professionals who show under popular judges year after year gain familiarity with them. But then so do the dedicated owner-handlers who show the product of their breeding programs generation after generation. The judge will think, here comes so-and-so. She's been going to a lot of shows for a lot of years. She generally brings good dogs. Let's see what she has to show to me today.

The same holds true for a good professional who has shown a string of good dogs over many years. The judge will be curious to see what that handler has to show. That name and face recognition will carry an exhibitor, whether amateur or professional, through the initial impression in the show ring, but a good judge will make an evaluation despite the fact that he or she knows the exhibitor. It's called paying your dues, and you are learning presentation at the same time.

PICTURES AND GIFTS

Don't take a picture with a judge unless it is someone you respect, or unless it is a particularly big win. It is perfectly acceptable to send a picture of the win to the judge. Some of them really like to keep a record of the dogs they have put up, and many judges have folders or scrapbooks of their days in the ring.

It is not necessary to thank a judge for a win. When you send the picture, you might include a little note saying something like, "We thought you might like to have this picture of a day that was special to us." Do not send it with the life history or complete show record of the dog. Do not send flowers or gifts. That puts judges in a compromising situation. Certainly do not ever send a judge pictures of your dog before a show. Any judge worth a nickel will throw the picture away and send you directly to last place. Don't carry around scrapbooks of your dog and attempt to corral the judge into looking at them. This is one of the least classy things you can do to promote your dog, although some people seem to get away with it.

FRIENDSHIPS IN THE RING

There is a great deal of controversy about the propriety of showing to one's friends, or even acknowledging that one knows the judge. Some of this has been taken to the extreme. Suppose you are well acquainted with a judge because you have shown to this person many times before, or even because you have been at some of the same social events. For appearances' sake, it is best to be casual and brief in your conversations with that judge if you should meet prior to going into the ring. Exhibitors who hang around the judge, either before or after the breed is completed, show extremely poor taste and put the judge in an awkward position.

Some judges do not like to have their friends show dogs to them. Exhibitors should be aware of this and respect that judge's feelings. Others do not care at all if they are friends with an exhibitor, because they will put up what they like regardless of relationships. The exhibitors, in those situations, must realize that they may lose. If you do not wish to lose under a friend, don't enter that show. Friendships should have nothing to do with honest judging, but unfortunately in the real world they do. The American Kennel Club is very specific about certain restrictions, such as relatives or former clients showing to judges, but in other instances it really is a matter of common sense and good taste. If it doesn't feel right to you, don't do it for the sake of a ribbon.

Judges are people, too. They have personalities just like everybody else in this world. Make judges your friends, using the criteria you would use for anyone else. Most judges see through the facade of fake friendships for the sake of winning, which in the long run will do you more damage than good.

GOOD SPORTS

True *professional* handlers are generally good sports. You will always see losers congratulating winners in the Group ring. They will most often go out of their way to help their competitors outside the ring. Although their livelihood depends on winning with their dogs, human relationships are important and they will rally around if the need arises. Owner-handlers sometimes are not as charitable, either as winners or as losers.

Good sportsmanship is an important lesson to be learned in presenting a dog properly. If you are going to show dogs over a period of many years, you will find it far more enjoyable to be known as a good sport than as a sore loser. Many lasting friendships are made at dog shows. Sportsmanship and a sense of perspective about what is really important in and out of the show ring help foster those relationships.

11

Planning a Campaign

$\mathbf{P}$LANNING A CAMPAIGN means exactly that—planning in advance for exactly how you will proceed to show this dog as a Specials exhibit.

EVALUATING YOUR DOG

We will assume that you will start with a dog that is already finished. It may be a year old, two or even three years of age and either a dog or a bitch. The first thing you must do is to honestly evaluate the dog. You have to look at both the faults and the good points of your dog and determine whether the good points outweigh the bad. Are the good points things that can be accentuated in presentation, such as a beautiful head, proper expression, excellent topline or whatever the emphasis in the Standard is for your breed?

Can the faults be easily disguised or adjusted so that they will not overcome the dog's good points? *This does not mean artificially altering your dog by surgically correcting a fault or dyeing to change the color.* The dog must have natural attributes that you feel are worthy of presenting to the dog fancy.

Is the dog a "looker"? This means, does your dog look at objects other than you to concentrate on? The dog with the longest concentration span will be the better show dog. While you are playing with your dog at home, or just watching the dog move and stand in the backyard, does it focus on things with intensity?

Evaluate how your dog moves on its own and how it stands without being stacked, because the more naturally correct the dog is, the less compensating you will have to do in the ring. It may be that the dog moves beautifully around the backyard but looks terrible on a lead. You know the potential is there, but it will be your job to teach your dog to move just as effortlessly on a lead in the ring. You must be able to get the dog to gait and stack for the best-looking presentation. This may take a month or a year to accomplish.

When you initially look at your dog, determine the type of hair that it has. If it is a coated breed, decide if you will be able to sell this hair—the quality, length color and markings—to the judge. On a coated breed, such as an English Springer or Irish Setter, the initial trim should be done over a period of two to three months. Don't even try to Special a dog if it is in poor condition, out of coat, over- or underweight or flabby.

Take a series of photos when you win so that you can see what your dog looks like and where the grooming might be different. You can see through pictures whether the dog would look better being stacked in a different way or whether it needs to put on or take off weight.

The evaluation of your dog is an ongoing process that lasts the whole career of the dog. The dog changes muscle, ligaments, hair and mental attitude, and you have to adapt your method of presentation to all these changes to constantly improve what your dog looks like.

You may have to emphasize different areas as the dog matures, or to downplay certain features, such as head, front, topline or hindquarters, as the dog's physiology changes.

Dogs at different ages should be shown at different weights. At an older age they cannot carry as much weight as they can in their prime. You must constantly observe your dog and be able to take off or put on a couple of pounds of the dog's weight as needed. Evaluation of your dog's mental and physical condition continues throughout the dog's entire career.

GOALS

Once you have decided that you have a dog good enough to campaign as a Special, you will want to set some goals for yourself and for the dog. A person has to realistically decide what they expect the dog to do. To be considered one of the top dogs in the country, the dog would have to win the Breed 90 percent of the time it is shown and the Group 50 percent of the time it wins the Breed. It must go Best in Show at least once out of every four times that it competes in that ring.

You must decide what interests you the most. Is it winning Breeds, or winning Breeds and placing in the Group? Will you be happy with a Group 2 or 3 or 4, or is your goal to rack up the greatest number of Group 1s? Your goals will depend somewhat on the breed you are showing. Because of the level of competition in the breed and the visibility of that breed in the Group, you should tailor your goals to realistic expectations. For instance, the owner of a rare breed would be happy with one Group 4 during a year because that breed almost never gets attention on the Group level. On the other hand, an English Springer Spaniel, Irish Setter or Standard Poodle that won a Group 4 during the course of a year would be a noncontender.

You might decide to go for the greatest number of Breed wins and concentrate on the Breed level rather than the Group level for your dog. You have to remember, too, that judges judge differently on the Group level than they do at the Breed level, so your dog may do nicely in the breed but not well in the Group. You will know this after you have been out a while, and you might decide to concentrate your efforts in that direction.

You also must evaluate the competition in the breed at the time you are starting to campaign your dog. If it happens to be a time when there is no one big winner, you have an advantage when you first start out because you will not immediately be perceived as the potential giant killer.

FINANCES

Campaigning a dog is expensive. There is no getting away from that fact. Entry fees, travel, lodging, food, catalogs and advertising all add up to a pretty sizable amount of money. You may have to figure out in advance how much you want to spend during the course of a year and adjust your campaign goals to fit your budget. You can do it without advertising, but usually advertising is part of the campaign package. You will need to decide if you can afford to show straight down the line every weekend all year long, or whether your goals should fit a less demanding and less expensive schedule. You should plan for the maximum that you can do at the start, and then evaluate your progress and the development of your dog to see if your level of achievement is worth the money you are spending on that dog.

STRATEGY

When you start your dog off, the first thing you want to do is to make a list of specific judges for whom you have respect. Not necessarily those with whom you agree, but those whose opinions you value. Good handlers have four to six judges that they use as a test, very similar to the way companies test market a product. They know that if judge A likes their dog, that there are others who judge in similar fashion, and they can add about twenty additional judges to their original test list.

A handler may take a dog to judge B, who in the past may not have liked their particular type of dog, but may like this one for one reason or another. It may have a head, eye, topline or whatever that pleases judge B. The handler then adds another group of judges to judge B's type. This is done for all the test judges on your list.

The goal of test marketing a dog is to see who is going to like it. Are breeder judges going to appreciate your dog, are all-rounders or judges who are movement-conscious, head-hunter judges or front-movement judges? You won't know until you go through your list of test judges. Even though your dog may not have the greatest head in the world, it may be passable enough so that if a judge who is a ''head hunter'' likes the rest of the dog enough, the dog will win. The same strategy may hold true for any other part of the dog, including movement.

While you are test marketing your dog, you will find judges who will like your dog and those who will not. If a judge does not

Ch. Mr. Stewart's Chesire Winslow winning his first Group. Notice the hard stack.

Best in Show—free-stacked and at the prime of his career.

like the dog the first time, go back and try that judge a second and possibly a third time.

As an example, there was a handler who showed an Irish Setter to a judge and was defeated in the Breed on Sunday. The following Sunday that judge put the dog Best in Show over 3,700 entries. In another situation a handler was beaten three times in the Breed by the same judge. The fourth time the judge gave the dog Group 1 at Westminster.

Judges can only evaluate what is in the ring on a given day. Although a judge may not like your dog and would defeat it if there was something more to his or her liking in the ring, sometimes that is just not possible. A judge may have no choice but to put your dog up over the others because he considers it the best of a bad lot. That may be damning with faint praise. But in winning, the judge has considered yours against the others. If you conditioned and presented your dog better, you will have a decided edge.

In another instance your dog may not have been showing at its best, and the next time you show to that judge it may look completely different.

Maturity plays a big part in how a judge views your dog. It may have been an ugly teenager that grew into a beautiful adult in the time between the first loss and the first win from that judge.

Some judges are adamant about exhibitors who do not follow instructions and, in a close decision, will penalize someone to the extent of denying a win if they do not pay attention. The next time the exhibitor will know better, and if the judge likes the dog, she will put it up.

At prestigious shows, such as Westminster and Santa Barbara, psychology has a lot to do with how some judges behave in the ring. They are always under great pressure to do a good job, to pick the best dog, and sometimes in the effort to do that, they judge differently than they normally do. In a class of excellent specimens, such as one finds in Group and Best in Show lineups at big shows, judges may begin to pick on faults rather than good points of the exhibits. They may end up with a dog they would not normally choose, but by nit-picking the parts they end up with a dog that may not have been to their liking at all on a different day.

Some judges, especially those who are out in the rings every weekend of the year, do play politics in the ring. Dogs who compete in the same region week after week often come up to the same judges in Group and Best In Show rings. If a judge has given one dog important wins several times in a row, he or she may choose to go with another dog just to spread the honors around more evenly. Judges do not like to be considered biased towards one dog or one handler.

Judges are human, too, and their opinions are just that—opinions of your dog on any given day.

EVALUATING YOUR PRESENTATION

When you start campaigning your dog, you have to evaluate the competition that you are competing against, first on the breed level. You have to come up with a philosophy of presentation that you would like to achieve.

You want to be different in order to set your dog apart from the competition, but not so different that the judge will have to make a choice between black and white.

For example: a dog who is shown gaiting at a fast pace compared to the dog shown very, very slowly. It may be proper for the breed to be shown at a slower pace, but perhaps the top winning dog in that breed has been flying around the ring for two or three years. Judges have come to expect those dogs to fly. Even though it may go against your principles to show your dog that way, you will have to start your campaign showing your dog at a fast pace.

When you begin to win consistently, you may change your actions to better suit your own philosophy of what that breed should look like. This is true of stacking, grooming and trimming as well as gaiting.

Your dog must look enough like the others so that the judge will have to stop and evaluate it and not have the chance to dismiss it because it is different. If the initial presentation looks as if it comes close to the big-winning dog of the day, then the judge will have to consider it. However, don't simply copy what the other handler is doing, because that person will do it better. The other handler-dog team has been at it longer and has the routine perfected. You should come close to the same philosophy of presentation so that the judge will have something to compare.

When the English Springer Spaniel Ch. Salilyn's Private Stock began his career, he was shown on a tight lead and at a slower speed

Ch. Salilyn's Private Stock, a multiple Best in Show winner, shown here in his prime. Note the similarities in presentation between Stock in his prime and Stuart in his.

Ch. Telltale Royal Stuart at the beginning of his career—14 months. Note the exaggerated topline and length of neck.

Stuart six months later. You can see the maturity of body and less extreme presentation.

Stuart winning Best of Breed from the Veterans' class in 1989. Notice the difference in both dog and method of presentation from the beginning to the end of his career.

135

than I would have preferred. His coat was trimmed tighter and he was stacked with an extreme topline, although that is not the way I believe a Springer should be shown. However, the competition was being presented that way.

Once the dog started to win, I was gradually able to show the dog in a more compact, less extreme stack. He grew a longer topcoat and undercoat, and the dog was gaited on a dropped loose lead. These changes took place over a two-year period. I went from a presentation I did not agree with to one of showing and grooming that breed in the way I think it should be done.

Exactly the same procedure was used in the presentation of the Springer Ch. Telltale Royal Stuart. He began his career being shown with an extreme topline and exaggerated neck and shoulders. What he looked like at the beginning is totally different from how he appeared at the end of his career. Again, once we became the ones to beat, it was easier to set the style for others to follow and show the dog the way I truly felt to be the most appropriate.

We used the same technique for the Irish Setter Am. & Can. Ch. McCamon Marquis, who was shown in the United States for the first time when he was just under two years old and finished his campaign at under five years of age.

Sometimes the differences in development and presentation are so dramatic that you would think that they are different dogs when early and late pictures are displayed. The two photos of Ch. Glendee's Stone Cutter, the first taken in March of 1981 and the last in November 1982, show a totally different dog. The method of grooming, the development of the dog physically and the presentation were changed dramatically over a year and a half.

The top winning Great Pyrenees Ch. Rivergrove's Run For The Roses was shown over an extended period of time. The first photo, taken early in the dog's career, shows an entirely different dog than one taken three years later. The later picture shows a dog much more developed in body and coat, shown and groomed to emphasize the mature qualities of the dog.

STARTING THE CAMPAIGN

In the beginning of the campaign, do not show your dog more than three times in one month. While you are test marketing, show

Ch. Glendee's Stone Cutter at the start of his career.

Ch. Glendee's Stone Cutter 21 months later.

once during a weekend and then take a week off. Occasionally you may want to show twice in a weekend, with a week or even two weeks in between outings.

Remember that you are going into the ring with the idea that the dog will enjoy the entire experience. Your biggest concern should be that the dog be happy and confident in the ring. At the same time you will be listening to the judge's comments. Don't ask for opinions. Usually a judge will offer comments if he or she likes a dog, even if you do not win under that judge. The judge may tell you the dog needs to be slowed down or speeded up, needs more hair or more body or whatever the comment may be. Listen and evaluate, but do not argue with the judge. You may not agree with the opinion, but factor it into your thinking.

During the week take the dog in the car, go to McDonald's and buy your dog a hamburger. The dog will soon learn that riding means good things happen, and will be mighty upset at being left home, especially on those occasions that you go to shows and don't take your best friend along.

During the period in which you are showing sporadically, try to get feedback from people in your breed and from other handlers. If your dog is good enough, people will come up and tell you what they think. Sometimes they will even tell you if they think your dog is a bum. You want people to talk about your dog while you listen. Do not brag about your dog. Let performance speak for itself.

Do not ever start a rigorous campaign in the first part of the year from February to May. This is the time you want to take it easy, test market your dog and evaluate its performance.

Do not start any kind of campaign from May until September. In the spring you may want to take your dog to one or two shows a month, but in the summer heat never do two shows on a weekend. You want to see how the dog withstands the heat without pushing and without worrying about winning.

We want the dog to have at least nine months of consistent campaigning before we hit the hot shows. By then you will know the right buttons, what is good for the dog, what is not good and how to appease the dog who hates the heat. If you get a dog to love showing enough, mental attitude will bypass the heat and your dog will be able to fight through it. If the dog does not know what to do, performance will suffer. The dog should understand why it is being carted around in 110 degree weather.

In order to do this you must bring the dog along slowly, similar to the way baseball players are put into the minor leagues at the beginning of their careers and are brought along, watched and evaluated for their strengths and weaknesses. When they arrive in the big leagues, players are aware of what is expected of them and what their limitations are. Managers are thus able to adapt their players to the best roles for them. This is the same basic philosophy that should be used in starting a top show dog.

What you are aiming for is a dog that on the last day of a long career will give you the best show ever, with the most enthusiasm, the most heart, the most drive.

PICTURES CHART PROGRESS

From the time you begin your campaign you should have show pictures taken of your wins, not to advertise or to send around to the judges, but so that you have an accurate record of your dog's progress. After about six months, lay them all out on a table and view what changes have been made, whether the dog has gotten into bad habits, needs to be trimmed differently or stacked differently, and to see how the dog has developed physically.

You should be doing this throughout the dog's entire show career, from beginning to end. This could be especially helpful if the dog had been winning consistently and suddenly stopped winning. If you have a record in pictures you can see what changes transpired to cause this to happen. You may want to return to the method of grooming and presentation that was used during the dog's most successful period. Sometimes handlers allow bad habits to creep in without being aware of them. Pictures can tell the story and enable the handler to identify the problem and correct it.

Videos can be used as a tool, but not an absolute. What you see in a video is two-dimensional. The judge views your dog in three dimensions. Also, videos can be deceiving. What you see on a video may not be the same as what you see in real life.

ADVERTISING

Does advertising help a dog win more shows? Obviously a lot of owners think so, because dog magazines survive only with their

Ch. Rivergrove's Run For The Roses as a young dog in 1986.

Ch. Rivergrove's Run For The Roses as a mature dog in 1989.

These photos chart the dog's progress from the beginning through his career as a top Working Group contender.

140

support. Ask some judges and they will claim they never look at the ads. Others will admit to "glancing through" from time to time, and others admit that they read the ads, especially to see their own pictures in back of the dogs. Does that influence their judging decisions? No judge would admit that ads play a role, but just as with any product advertising, from toilet paper to new cars, brand recognition is the desired effect.

Ads can be tasteful or tacky. Advertising should be done not to gain wins in the future, but to brag about wins that already have happened. Advertise a win that you are proud of, under a judge for whom you have respect.

Don't demean judges by calling them "knowledgeable, most respected, highly regarded," or all those other oily adjectives that judges hate. Don't list every judge that ever gave your dog a class win.

Don't use advertising to plead for a win, such as "Looking for a major to finish." The judge will be looking, too, right to the end of the line.

There are many dogs who have gone through their whole careers with no advertising at all. The Great Pyrenees mentioned previously won every honor in the breed. He was the top Working Dog in the country, won the National Specialty multiple times and all that winning was done with not one ad.

The Doberman Pinscher bitch that won Best in Show at West-minster went through her whole career with no more than four ads during the year.

The top Newfoundland breeder in the country produces generations of winning dogs and campaigns them with practically no advertising.

On the other hand, many people advertise heavily to promote their dogs. Obviously they believe it works, or they would not be spending all that money.

If you decide to advertise, it should be done on a consistent basis. Not every week. Ads can be placed every two weeks or monthly, depending on your budget, and they should be used to project an image of you and your dog together.

Advertise a different win each time, but all the ads should have a similar format and promote the picture of you and your dog. If there is something outstanding or unique about the dog, you may decide to promote that. You might create a logo based on the dog's name or some attribute of the dog. You may create a picture that carries over into the ring that will instantly identify you with the dog.

One gentleman always showed his Great Danes wearing a Sherlock Holmes hat. In his advertising he was shown wearing the hat, so that when he came into the ring he was recognizable at once. A lady owner handler always wore a Robin Hood hat with a feather stuck into it. Still another wears cowboy hats in the ring and always in the advertising pictures. You might wear a trademark colored jacket or tie. Whatever it is, you can build your advertising campaign around that identifiable attribute.

Do not waste your money putting a single ad in a publication just prior to a very important show. If you have not built name recognition by then, it is too late. Some people advertise a win under a judge just before that judge is about to see the dog at a very prestigious show, such as the National Specialty. This can have a very negative effect on the judge and should be avoided at all costs. Judges do not like to be reminded in print what they have done in the hope they will be encouraged to repeat the win.

Do not ever publish a picture of your dog if the picture is bad, no matter how important the occasion. People want to see what your dog looks like, and if it is awful, that's what they will remember. I do not advise advertising Reserve wins or second place wins of anything. You never want to advertise your dog going second to somebody. You are better off publishing a Best of Breed picture than a Second in the Group, in my opinion. The only exceptions to this would be some of the rare breeds in which any Group win can be considered a great accomplishment.

CREATING THE IMAGE

If a small child handling an Irish Wolfhound wins a breed or a Group, that sight becomes instantly recognizable because it is unique. Once that child becomes noteworthy because of that accomplishment, every time the child enters the ring he or she will be recognized. The dog and the child would become an image.

One handler showed a Foxhound which he had trained to show itself. The handler never stacked the dog, and for that breed it was unique. The two created an image, instantly recognizable in the ring, and consequently in any advertising that was done for the dog.

If you do something about the way you wear your hair, keep it the same every time. Bring out something interesting about your dog. There was a Bichon Frise who did a lot of winning, as much on her personality as on her conformation. She would leap into the air, barking and wagging her tail at the end of every gaiting pattern. She became well known with her handler for the picture they made in the ring.

CONTINUING THE CAMPAIGN

Once you have done a test marketing and have found out what kind of judges are going to like the dog—what basic judging philosophy the dog appeals to—then show as often as you can, straight down the line. This follows the adage "Absence makes the heart grow fonder of somebody else." The only exception to this is if you know a judge in your area hates your dog.

TRAVEL

The amount of travel you do to campaign your dog will depend upon the amount of time and money you have available to show your dog and upon the goals you wish to attain. It has become a fact that in order to become one of the top dogs in the country, you have to add up as many frequent flyer miles as you do points on your dog.

If you have a good dog, unless you live in a remote section of the country, you should be able to find shows within a reasonable distance of your home almost every weekend of the year. It is much less wearing on you and the dog not to fly around the country, and it is extremely bad form to chase judges from one end of the country to another in search of a win. If your dog is good enough, it should be able to win in any competition, not only in West Wazoo.

ENDING A CAMPAIGN

A campaign usually lasts two years, sometimes three, depending upon the breed and the success of the dog in competition.

If you consider that it takes six to nine months to start your campaign and then two years to actively show the dog, you will have had sufficient time to reach whatever goals you have set. Sometimes a dog can go three years, but that takes a really special type of dog, and usually by the end of that time the dog is past its peak.

Know when to stop. It is better to quit with your dog on top than down and dragging like a punch-drunk fighter. Owner-handlers sometimes get so caught up in winning one more Group or one more Specialty or one more Best in Show that they forget about the dog. If your dog has shown its heart out for you, you owe it to your dog to retire with dignity at top form. The dog will be remembered as a winner and you will be remembered as a good sport, good dog person and good competitor.

12

Helpful Hints

GROOMING

1. Always use toenail clippers when trimming the nails. There are two basic kinds, the guillotine type and the pincher type. Whichever you use, be sure the cutting edge is kept sharp or the nails will tear, rather than be cut cleanly. Do not use a grinder which is available as an addition to some electric clippers because you may not be able to tell when you are getting into the quick and hurting the dog. However, some dogs are so fussy about their feet, that a grinder is the only thing they will tolerate.

2. Never brush a dry coat. Always dampen the coat with a mist of water or water and conditioner which you spray onto the brush before brushing the dog. Brushing the coat dry will split the ends of the hair. Use a soft bristle brush on short coated breeds and on those with flat silky top coats. When you brush double coated dogs or those with long fine hair, brush from the skin out in small sections, lifting the coat with one hand and brushing with the other.

3. Do not use a hairdryer on the top coat of some Sporting breeds because you will dry out the hair. Use a dryer on

the feathering and only on the blow or warm air cycle. Never use a hot blower on any coat because it will dry and split the hair.

4. Do not rub conditioning into the coat as it will clog the pores of the skin. Apply only as a rinse according to the type of hair and the effect you wish to achieve.

5. Trim for the show ring two days after bathing in order for you to be able to see how the coat lies. Then bathe again just prior to the show and do final touch-up trimming the day before a show. Dogs being shown should be bathed once a week, and those with feathering should have the feathers washed every day. This is especially important for males who soil their belly coat and legs when they urinate. A heavier conditioner can be used on these areas during the week.

6. Do not use silicone-based products on the coat during hot weather. They conduct heat and will burn the dog's coat. If you use these products as conditioners during the week they must be washed off every few days or they will break the hair.

HANDLING TIPS IN REVIEW

1. Apply HEET or Vicks Vapor Rub to the lead to prevent the dog from chewing on it. Dogs will chew from boredom or because they want to get out of the situation they are in. Training the dog to respect the lead is an even better solution than by artificial means.

2. Walking is better exercise for a show dog than galloping because it is controlled exercise and the muscles are the same muscles and the same pattern of gait as are used when trotting in the ring.

3. Some people use a jogger or trotter to exercise their dogs. These must be used with caution. Some dogs love it once they are used to it. Others hate it and will fight it all the way. These dogs cannot be put on the jogger because they might injure themselves. A dog must be started slowly on a jogger and *never* before it is fully mature. Two minutes

at the beginning is sufficient. For those dogs who do not mind it, try putting a fan in front of the dog so it thinks it is heading into the wind.

4. To wear a dog down, stand outside the ring for a long time. How many times have you seen people standing around ringside with their dogs for an hour ahead of time. These are not dogs that need calming, so by the time they get into the ring they are dead on their feet. However, for a hyperactive dog, waiting at ringside can take the edge off.

5. To determine when to bring your dog up to the ring, watch the judging from the beginning of the assignment and time how long it takes the judge to complete a class. Count the number of dogs ahead of your class and factor in any lunch break that the judge may have scheduled. If you are in doubt about this, ask the ring steward.

   If yours is the first class, watch the judge if he or she is doing a breed just prior to yours so that you will know how long it takes to judge a class.

6. Ask for or pay for advice. If you do this the person you are asking will know that you are sincerely interested in learning about a specific thing. Do not take unasked for advice because it is usually wrong or inappropriate for your dog. Occasionally a knowledgeable person will offer advice if they think you have a promising dog that is not being groomed or handled properly. Factor this information in with others you receive before following it.

7. The judge gives points at the end of the class, not at the beginning. Therefore, do not push your dog to perform to its maximum effort the moment you step into the ring.

8. To teach a dog to gait ahead of you, practice getting the dog to look for objects, such as a ball or a towel that you use to play with. Teach the dog to seek or find things that you have placed ahead of it. Use a command, such as "Find it," or "Get it," as you start your gaiting pattern.

9. Teach a dog to retrieve and your dog will focus on anything you say in the show ring. You can get the dog to look alert, ears up and tail out or up just by telling the dog to "Look at" or "See."

10. If at all possible, practice handling skills on a dog that is not being shown. If you are starting off with a new dog, use the older one to work with. An older dog will forgive your mistakes. Perhaps a friend will let you work with one of theirs so that you do not get your puppy into bad habits and make it dislike the whole business.

11. Always have a reason for anything you do in the show ring. Use your mental facilities to plan every move. If it doesn't have a good reason, don't do it. Most owner-handlers spend a great deal of time in the ring fiddling unecessarily with their dogs. This only wears them out and gets them bored and disinterested. It also builds up nervous energy which transmits right down the lead to the dog.

12. Don't copy another handler's methods without a reason. Professionals usually have reasons for doing what they do in the ring with a particular dog. It may not be right for your dog and if you copy what they are doing, you will make your dog look bad, while their dogs look better. Don't fall into the trap of imitation.

13. If a dog sidewinds when gaiting on the left side, train it by gaiting it on the right side. Often a dog will learn to sidewind if it looks up at the handler for bait, or if the handler cannot run in a straight line. In addition to gaiting on the right side, you can train it by running along a wall or a fence so that the dog has no room to swing its hindquarters out.

    A dog who is structurally unbalanced may sidewind if the rear angulation is greater than the front so that when the dog reaches ahead with its rear legs they must pass outside or inside of the front legs. The only way to compensate for this is to adjust the rate of speed the dog is traveling. Some dogs sidewind less if gaited at a slower speed. Others do better going faster. You have to experiment with your dog.

14. To make a dog stand still when it is moving its feet, push it off balance just a little. It will not like the feeling of insecurity and will plant its feet pretty firmly after that.

15. To get the dog to turn in the direction you want it to, train by using Obedience About Turns. Gather the lead in your

hand so that the dog is close to your side and reverse your direction, turning either right or left, keeping the dog next to you. Teach the dog to follow you by giving praise and encouragement.

16. You should be able to feel without looking if your dog is not standing or moving correctly. Practice stacking your dog while wearing a blindfold. Then remove the blind and see how well you have done. In order to do this properly you must know your dog's anatomy very well. You should be able to feel where the shoulder blades are, where the rear legs stand when the hocks are perpendicular to the ground. Then you must develop the sensitivity to realize when the lead moves or when a foot moves out of position.

17. Control of the dog's head will determine how the dog will distribute its weight and use a center of gravity. Practice holding the head at different angles, up, out or down, so that you can see how this affects different parts of the body. This is true both for stacking and for gaiting. A dog will gait differently with its head held up than it will if the head reaches forward.

18. The most important time in the presentation of your dog is when the judge approaches. At that moment you must have your dog looking perfect. All the practice in stacking and subtly showing off the best aspect of your dog must be brought into play then. You have only a few seconds to make that impression, so all your psychic energy must be used at that time.

19. If the dog constantly shakes its head before it begins gaiting, blow in one ear. However, outside the ring you had better check the condition of the dog's ears. Dogs with ear infections will be seriously bothered by the lead around their necks. Another medical cause for head shaking could be swollen tonsils. It is surprising how many dogs are shown with ear or throat problems which the owners have overlooked.

Sometimes dogs are bothered by the sound of a choke chain, so if you have ruled out medical causes, use another type of collar.

20. It is easier to bring a dog's level of enthusiasm down than it is to bring it up. A dog with plenty of go-power can be

brought under control a lot easier than it would be to psych up a dog who is basically a deadhead. Dogs who lack enthusiasm for the show ring must be brought along very carefully in order to nurture and reinforce whatever good experiences they have had.

21. Puppies often get carsick up to the age of eight months. This has to do with the development of the bones of the inner ear. Usually by that time the condition passes. Sometimes, however, puppies have had such bad experiences with sickness while traveling that they carry those associations over for a long time. This is not a good situation for a show dog who spends much of its life on the road.

    During the developing stage of a puppy's life, keep trips short, if possible. Try different places in the car. Some dogs get sick in the back, but not in front. With others it makes no difference. Some home remedies which sometimes work are: feed a small amount of honey just before traveling. Or, give a couple of ginger snaps. It is the ginger, apparently, which helps calm the stomach.

22. To keep a dog's feet from sliding on slippery floors or mats apply a small amount of Classic Coca Cola to the pads of the feet. It is the sugar syrup which helps the feet stick to the floor. There are a couple of commercial products on the market which make the feet less slippery, but they are not good for the dogs if they are ingested. Unless you plan to wash your dog's feet immediately after showing it, Coca-Cola is safer.

23. To keep a dog from panting, apply one drop of lemon juice to the tongue. The puckery effect will make a dog close its mouth temporarily. On an extremely hot day, however, the dog must pant in order to get rid of heat in the body. It is cruel and dangerous to try to keep a dog's mouth closed continuously.